FORGETFUL HEART

Remembering God in a Distracted World

LUCY MILLS

DARTON · LONGMAN + TODD

First published in 2014 by
Darton, Longman and Todd Ltd
1 Spencer Court
140–142 Wandsworth High Street
London SW18 4JJ

ISBN 978-0-232-53071-1

A catalogue record for this book is available from the British Library.

Designed and phototypeset by Judy Linard
Printed in Turkey by Imak Ofset

FORGETFUL
HEART

For Mum and Dad

Contents

Acknowledgements

There are many who have shared this journey with me and given me support along the way. They include Bev Geen, dear friend and coffee companion; Sarah Erskine, kindred spirit extraordinaire; Kaye Seaward, who let me write at her kitchen table; Rachel Ford; Gwyneth Tonkin and Rachel (Ray) Reynolds – thanks for your enthusiasm and encouragement.

I'm indebted to the team at *Magnet* magazine for their support and training, giving me insight into the editor's eye-view. I'm particularly appreciative of Lynne Ling and Ann Barlow, who have been so interested in my writing and have shown such delight at the publication of *Forgetful Heart.*

I've been greatly helped by members of the Association of Christian Writers, in particular those with whom I've served on the committee: Merrilyn, Corin, Sam, Rob, Eric, Joe, Marion, Angela, Brian, Adrianne, Mandy and formerly Jenn – thank you. I'm extra grateful to Rob Chidley for taking such time and care in going over my book proposal. Thanks also to Jan Greenough for taking me aside at a Writers' Day and telling me I qualified to go to the 'experienced writers' session! Annie Porthouse has been ready to reassure me as I've gone through the process of getting published. I'm so pleased to have the chance to get to know her better, now that we are members of the same church!

Folks at Thornhill Baptist Church are too many to mention – you've seen me from wannabe-writer to published writer and I've been touched by your enthusiasm. Special mentions go to Ruth and James Neve, John and Beryl Vaughan, Tim and Judy Dennis, Liz and Nick Warn … I could go on.

Thanks also go to Chard Baptist Church for being so welcoming, and to St Augustine's, Heanton Punchardon, whose magazine featured some of my earliest writing attempts!

Other encouragers have hailed from Connexion, an organisation supporting those married to Baptist ministers – Lori Brighton in particular has been a real encouragement on my writing journey.

There are those who have taken time to look some of the

book's content in draft form: thanks to Amy Boucher Pye for being so interested and enthusiastic. David Kinchin gave valuable input at the later stages of writing the book. Huge appreciation goes to Conrad Gempf for feedback and for friendship – it's meant a lot.

Thanks to those who visit my website, read and comment on my blog and communicate via Twitter and Facebook – I couldn't name you all so I will send a virtual group hug your way (or handshake, if you prefer!).

I'm so pleased to be working with the lovely people at DLT, publishers of *Forgetful Heart*. Will Parkes was my 'first contact' at DLT and was enthusiastic from the start – big thanks to him. And more to Helen Porter and David Moloney – for encouragement, inspiration and patience with all my questions! Thank you to Kathy Dyke for being so diligent and sensitive in editing the manuscript.

I'm grateful for the support of my wider family (a special mention to Uncle Peter and the rat, although I may be the only one who remembers the context!).

Margaret and Mike Mills – thank you for welcoming me as daughter-in-law and being so affirming and proud of my writing endeavours. I very much appreciate it.

Deborah, David, Jonathan, Louise, Josh and Sam – my brothers and sisters and two fantastic nephews are a source of great encouragement to me, at all times in life. Debbie Goode and Richard Irwin – thanks for being such great siblings-in-law! Special thanks to Deborah Cheesman who has been particularly supportive of me as a writer as well as a sister.

Mum and Dad – you've always believed in me and never laughed at my dreams. You are a constant support and I can't put a value on your unconditional love. Thank you.

Andy, my husband – you recognised I was a writer even before I raised the subject! You have been my partner and chief companion on this journey. You made this book possible. I love you.

There are many others I could have mentioned who have played starring roles in my life so far. I'm so grateful to God for you, and pray that I may always remember the love I have been shown.

Introduction

It's not just an age thing. Not for everyone. From my teens I've been climbing the stairs and then wondering why I went up in the first place. Perhaps it's to do with having a creative (cluttered) mind. Inevitably I'm thinking about a few things at once. Perhaps I'm mulling over something I heard recently, while trying to work out what to have for dinner. I might be thinking about the paragraph I'm intending to write next. All this while I'm going upstairs to fetch – what? It's gone. I end up going back down in order to remember why I came up. Embarrassingly, this can happen more than once. It's an irritating, if ordinary, forgetfulness.

But I also suffer from something much more serious. It's common, rife even, in our everyday lives. I don't just forget ordinary, trivial things. I forget about who I really am, and what has been done for me. I forget the One who made and redeemed me. I forget to love and be loved. I forget the things that are really important.

I confess.

I have a forgetful heart.

FORGETFUL HEART

*I spend
so many days
just passing you by
unintentional, perhaps –
I pay you lip service
sometimes, not even that.
the occasional nudge
of memory,
provoking an 'in a minute'
or 'maybe later'
forgetting even
to acknowledge you,
until some panic
makes me reach for you,
demand your help
when things collide
and get rather
messy.*

*but still, for some
reason I can't grasp,
you treasure me,
in all my half-heartedness
your flamboyant love
encases me
for a mere, tiny step
sees you running, delighted
to meet me.
and tomorrow
you remain unfailing,
despite the fact
I rarely learn
from my mistake
and so easily forget you.
but you never forget
I am etched into your hands,
marked with a value
I could never deserve.*

Part I
A Modern Virus

Chapter 1
Longing to Remember

My soul thirsts for God, for the living God.
When shall I come and behold the face of God?
Psalm 42:2

I struggle to remember. I sift through the clutter of my mind for that one thing I'm looking for, that which I sense I am missing. It assumes huge importance and makes me anxious, chiefly because I don't know how important it really was – or is.

I wish I could remember. I wish I could find what was lost.

A Talent for Forgetfulness
I try to keep track of things. I write to-do lists, but even here am somewhat hapless – I end up having lists that say 'see other list'. I tried to use a page-a-day diary for this purpose, rolling things over as needed. This worked well for a while, but then I accidentally took the diary into a different room, left it under a pile of other books and promptly forgot about it.

Remembering is not my forte.

But memory maps the landscape of our lives. It informs us; teaches us by experience, triggers emotional responses – both negative and positive. It impacts relationships and grounds us in reality. It affects behaviour and attitude. It influences decisions; it shapes character and personality. It inspires gratitude and fuels worship. It gives meaning to objects and experiences, creating associations with the present and connecting us to the past. No wonder my forgetfulness frustrates me!

Our memories tell us who we are and who we have been. Memory (and the loss of it) is a popular theme in fiction, film, poetry and lyrics for that very reason. There is a whole proliferation of self-help books for improving memory. It's an intrinsic part of our daily lives.

Memory also contributes to our lives of faith. We *remember* what we believe and why we believe it. Memory takes what we learn and continually reapplies it, so that we act and think differently. Beyond this individual perspective, memory underpins the great narratives of religious history, telling salvation stories of the past and building a sense of identity not just for individuals but for families, communities and nations.

Records of Remembering

Despite recognising this, I'm aware of how little attention I pay to the God I profess to believe in. I forget God: forget what God has told me, done for me, asked me to do. When I do remember, I wonder how I could have forgotten. I don't put God on my to-do list; that seems rather demeaning. Ironically, this can mean that God is the last thing on my mind.

Over the years, I've kept occasional personal diaries and journals. I frequently reflect on life and faith. Sometimes, I remember to write my thoughts down.

Sometimes.

Looking through old journals is informative. I discover things I don't recall experiencing, moments of great excitement or understanding. I'm surprised to see that something I thought I'd learned recently I had already realised once, years before.

Then forgotten.

We might talk of a top ten 'unforgettable moments', assure ourselves that we will always remember the acuteness of an experience, the details of special celebrations, the punch line of a joke. Later, we try and recall these moments and find that details have slipped away into a fog. Even if the ingredients of these memories are stored in our minds somewhere, retrieval gets gradually harder with disuse. When reminded of something by someone else we struggle to recall our own perspective on it. If we do manage to retrieve the information, it takes us by surprise. How could it have disappeared so completely from my conscious mind? Where has it *been* all this time?

Some of us are more forgetful than others but, generally, we underestimate our tendency to forget. We can't imagine *not* knowing how we felt, what was said in that all-important moment, all those things we imagined would change our lives.

I read back over my journals and re-learn old lessons, recalling the vibrancy of the previous experience and relishing new and deeper understanding as I remember it. Yet suddenly I am afraid: what else have I forgotten and *never written down*? Some things – thoughts, experiences, lessons learned – have been lost, perpetually locked by neglect in the back rooms of my mind until they have begun to deteriorate, leaving only traces behind them until, eventually, even those remnants are gone. This fills me with a similar sense of disquiet to the one I described at the beginning of this chapter: I suspect I've forgotten something, and I can't even remember whether it was important or not. What if it *was* important? Was there something I needed to do, or say? Why didn't I realise I should make an effort to keep the memory alive?

The Nature of Memory

In this book I will refer to the mechanisms of memory, but at the same time I recognise that for many of us the power of memory is not in the detail of what happens in our brains, but in the moments of recall and the triggers that lead us there. The smell of someone's perfume, a moment of profound and personal revelation, the kindness of a friend, the absence of a loved one.

Nevertheless, memory is a process – one that receives, stores and retrieves information. When we receive new information our minds process it and organise it, reflect and engage with it. They form new connections with what we already know. We behave differently because of this remembering.

Cognitive scientists are now saying that individual memories are not boxed up in our minds like pre-assembled jigsaw puzzles or books on a shelf, perfectly bound and ready to read. We don't fish out ready-made memories but re-make them every time – sounds, smells and images all coming together in the act of recall.[1]

We can, of course, get these pieces in the wrong places, confusing what happened when and who said what. Nonetheless, the essence of the picture as it is formed, however muddled, brings with it strong emotions – passion, sadness, joy. Memory is an integral part of the human experience. However fractured and confused, confined or subjective, it still propels feeling and informs thought.

When we remember, we take out pieces of information – past experiences or things we have learned – and re-examine them. We also adapt them, applying the memory of *then* to *now*, and vice versa. When we remember things about God, this too is applied and adapted. Hopefully this causes us to live more faithfully because we have remembered our identity from the pieces we've cradled in our minds – pieces of hope, compassion, knowledge – all combining to tell us who we are.

For Christians, our identity lies in Christ. We were created

---

[1] This theory of memory as 'constructed' is explored in Charles Fernyhough's *Pieces of Light: The New Science of Memory* (Profile Books, 2012).

in God's image, and in his Son the ultimate demonstration and mending of that image takes place. Jesus Christ is the one we seek to imitate, enabled by the Holy Spirit.

Life in Storage

Our society relies on the written and recorded word. We don't need to rely on our biological memories; we have diaries, smartphones, computers, Google, you name it. There's a whole host of fantastic ways of storing information and keeping important records. Everything is put in place so that we don't forget the dentist or a special occasion or to feed the fish.

Why make an effort to retain information, when we have so many other things to do it for us? There's so much going on. We often don't focus fully on individual things. There's nothing there to recall, because we never committed it to memory. We forget how to remember!

In recording all the little things we need to do, bigger things slide into the background. These are things we don't expect to forget. However, what do we mean by 'remembering'? What does it mean for us to remember *God*?

Do we say we 'remember' something just because it's stored somewhere in our minds? What about *active* remembering, an essential power of recall which means that we are constantly applying our memories to our lives? How much do we remember *explicitly*? We'll see later how this active recall has always been important to the people of God. The Bible frequently uses the language of remembering to talk about how we should live. Knowledge of our faith is not merely a checklist of things to learn. It needs constant revisiting. Otherwise one day we'll reach into the dusty recesses of our minds and not even remember what it was we were hoping to find.

A Duty or a Need?

Those who have professed Christianity for a long time can believe they have ticked the relevant boxes and don't need to explore their faith more deeply. Praying and reading the Bible are often perceived as duties rather than needs. But what we remember is essential to discovering who we are, and who we are meant to be.

This is just as true for those at an earlier stage of their faith journeys. If we simply brandish another list of duties, albeit a more 'spiritual' one, we bypass the heart of the matter. In order to know how to live, we need to know who we are. In order to know who we are, we need to draw close to the one who knows us better than we know ourselves. We find our identity in God. This needs to be reflected in our lives.

I find that I live my life with such a forgetful heart that I often do not reflect my God-identity. I'm usually fearful, constantly careless and frequently preoccupied with things that don't matter. I long for my life to be productive and to make a difference, but in reality I spend so much time just *wasting* time. I don't take advantage of what I've been given and don't reflect on what I've learned. I consign myself to weary mediocrity, occasionally feeling a flash of longing for something deeper, something better, something closer to the life I feel I should be living. A life marked with the power of remembering, remembering that is not divided or distracted but focused on the one who makes it all worthwhile.

The Joy of Remembering

I remember when I was in my teens hearing people's stories of how they came to faith. I felt distressed because I couldn't remember the time I had made my first commitment; I knew when it was and what had happened but could not recall the experience itself. As I grew in maturity, I recognised that my journey of faith had been a whole series of commitments, and not everyone has one single moment to which they can point. But at the time, it mattered to me. I decided to pour out my feelings before God. *I know this is silly, but I want to remember. This is upsetting me. Could you deal with this?* I consciously placed my feelings into God's hands. I asked only for peace, a sense of resolution in myself.

God is bigger than our prayers. At the time I enjoyed writing songs and often recorded them onto cassette tape (remember those?). A few days after I'd brought my turmoil to God, I'd run out of space on the current tape, and went to ask my mum if she had any spare old ones. While we were rifling through drawers, we discovered some recordings of the church camp we'd been to when I was seven. It was here I made my first commitment to the Jesus I'd loved for some time. Intrigued, I took some away to listen to it, song recording put aside.

I found the one bearing the very date of my commitment: the day I had consciously chosen to follow Jesus for myself. I listened to the talk while pottering around my bedroom. It was about the 'lukewarm' Christians of Laodicea, and it was a challenging talk in its own right.

At the end of the talk, the tape kept playing.

I stopped everything as I heard the preacher lead his listeners in a prayer of commitment – the same prayer I'd whispered while sitting on my mother's lap. I crawled to my knees in my bedroom and wept. I wept because the memory had been returned to me – the very words of that moment. I could feel myself saying the words. I said them again, ten years later. And I wept at the kindness of God, who had heard my prayer and responded to it in a way I had not ever imagined.

Memory matters to us, and we matter to God.

God's Grace in our Forgetting

The wonderful thing is that *our memory loss does not change what God has done for us*. Because we believe in a God who remembers us, we can be assured that our own forgetfulness does not erase what he has done or who he is. Yes, we are called to remember but we must hold fast to this: God will remember us, even if our minds betray us from the inside. Remembering helps us to live out our calling and to own our identity, but our remembering God is above and beyond all our powers of recall.

It is with this very important acknowledgement that we look to encourage ourselves to remember God and his ways more profoundly in the way we think, feel and live. Because although there are some memory losses we cannot fight, we can still encourage ourselves to find triggers that help us remember *who we are in Christ* in the most ordinary places.

What does it mean to remember (and forget) God in our daily lives? In this book I'll reflect on how remembering has been so important in the lives of our ancestors in the faith, and how it affects the world around us. I'll ask what can help us practise the art of remembering better. And I'll admit that, despite all of this, I still have a forgetful heart. But I want to remember. I *long* to remember.

Does that sound at all familiar? If so, you'll be interested in reading this book. If it doesn't sound familiar, perhaps it's still worth reading. You may discover something you never realised you had forgotten.

so often I forget you

you are my sun
the blazing light
by which I see

you are my air
the very breath
by which I live

so often I forget you

you are my water
you bring life
to barren ground

you are my food
you give me strength
and help me stand

so often I forget you

you are my dying and my living
my breaking and my mending
the reason for my being

and you always remember

FOR REFLECTION

- If you had to give an extended answer to the question 'who are you?', what would you say?
- Write down some of your most formative memories. Note what it is about them that makes them so powerful.
- Do you find it easy to remember God's presence and actions in your life, or does it require conscious effort? Why?

There are points of reflection at the end of each chapter of *Forgetful Heart*, some referring back to exercises in previous chapters. You may wish to keep a notebook or journal for this purpose.

I will call to mind the deeds of the LORD;
I will remember your wonders of old.
I will meditate on all your work,
and muse on your mighty deeds.
Psalm 77:11–12

Chapter 2
The Lure of the Memory Makers

'Other seeds fell among thorns, and the thorns grew up and choked them.'
Matthew 13:7

When I forget something, it's often because it's been crowded out. With my mind whirring with things that concern me, I skip from topic to topic in my thoughts. I get distracted by something I come across while I'm working, watching or reading, re-routing my thought patterns and taking me on a different journey from the one I intended. I'm lured away from the things I *say* are the most important, ending up mired in places I never meant to be.

The Memory Exchange
We talk about having 'bad' (poor) memories, but our long-term memories are supposedly almost limitless. However, the particular form of short-term memory (STM) which is sometimes called *working memory* can only hold a certain number of things at once. *Working memory* is conscious of what it remembers.[1] This could be something I did five minutes ago and am still thinking about; it could be something I've recalled out of long-term memory (LTM).

Short-term and long-term memories are distinctive but co-operative. When we are actively 'remembering' something, we pull things *out* of LTM to put them temporarily *back in* to working memory. Our present experience informs the old memory and what gets put back into LTM is slightly modified. The two work together,

[1] This is different from *sensory memory*, which is the process that retains information for mere seconds after it is received – for example, what we call upon when we weren't paying attention, but with effort can pull out the last sentence we heard in order to 'prove' we were listening. Actually, it doesn't prove anything of the sort!

as team members with different – but complementary – roles.[2]

Because our working memories can only hold so much information, some of it gets filtered out. Only some of it moves into LTM, where we can reach for it again. If I've got 'a lot on my mind' then I won't be able to recall it all. If I do remember it, it will only be as a kind of recognition, a sense of familiarity due to something I later come across. I certainly won't be able to recall it without some external trigger jogging my memory.

The other thing we need in order for this memory transfer to work is attentiveness, something we'll examine in more detail later. If we're not paying attention to something, this hampers the memory exchange. The original focus is pushed out or overwhelmed. It gets forgotten – or at least, our memories of it are fractured and frustratingly inadequate. If we do pay attention, we can recall details much more easily. Consider: you're following a certain television programme and are completely focused on the characters or participants, discussing them with friends or colleagues the next day. You remember well enough to hold very strong opinions about it. You retain it because you gave it your full attention. However, our attention is often divided, and when our minds are full of other thoughts, needs and desires, it's easy to get pulled off course.

Leaking Minds

Our world is busy with distraction. We write lists and fill in diaries because we know we won't recall everything we need to know. We stop mid-sentence when we've lost the thread of our thoughts, especially if new circumstances arise which shout so loudly that previous whispers can no longer be heard. Our minds fill up and spill over – in a manner of speaking, they leak.

If our working memories are processing all the new information we're receiving as well as recalling old information, it's not just that we're preventing ourselves from making new memories. *We're not recalling the memories we already have.* What are we allowing to clog up our minds, preventing us from recalling these things?

In the parable of the sower, Jesus spoke of seeds that fall on thorny ground – those that grow in faith but are choked by the cares and desires of the world. These cares crowd in and entangle the growing seedlings, dragging them down and blocking out the

---

[2] A good overview of the processes of memory can be found in *Memory: A Very Short Introduction* by Jonathan K. Foster (Oxford University Press, 2009). However, theories are shifting all the time!

light. The seedlings are stifled, cluttered, choked.[3] What are the things that choke our abilities to grow in our faith and remember what we have learned about God?

When Worry Takes Control

We don't think of worry as something that damages our capacity to remember because it so often repeats one story over and over again. But it's dangerously selective. Worries get bigger and spill over into other areas. Everything else gets trodden down, squeezed out and choked by their consuming power. Consider the Israelites in the wilderness, panicking over lack of water and food.[4] They took their present situation – no food, no water – and didn't marry it together with past experience of God's provision for them. *Past faithfulness is divorced from future reality by present forgetfulness.* When we're anxious, all we remember is the thing we're worrying about – it takes the main stage, and all that's left is the occasional bit part or background extra.

Worry very easily resurrects past problems. It forgets promises and reassurances. If we don't take time to draw close to God and remember what we know about God, we bow down to worry instead. The more we let it, the more it chokes us, the more distracted we become, and the more we forget the very person who is able to rescue us.

Stress Addicts

There's always so much to do, to think about, to get through. 'Keeping busy' has become a virtue. Somewhere along the line of making good use of our time and being diligent, we have become overloaded with all we need to do, all we want to do, and all we will never do but plan to do anyway. We come and we go, we walk and we run, we fill in the gaps with yet more distraction, things that *make us forget* the rest of life, for a while.

Escapism becomes the goal. Our next holiday. The weekend. Somewhere and some time when we can stop, get away. Our lists are full of things we need to remember, but they contain gaping holes. By the time we do stop, we find we've forgotten how to rest, how to slow our hearts and our minds. We are used to the busyness, the stressfulness, the constant quest for immediacy. We complain about these things, but we're not sure how to live without them.

[3] Matthew 13:7, 22.
[4] e.g. Numbers 21:5.

Are you a stress addict, accustomed to feeling harangued, pressured and busy? Do you feel there's something you should be doing, even if you can't tell what it is? Frequently I catch myself in this cycle and tell myself not to be so ridiculous. I would scold someone else for feeling this way, so why do I allow it in myself? I feel guilty for sitting down and doing nothing. I've had to learn to rest, to discipline myself to stop.

Resting is not as passive as it sounds. It takes practice. Addictions take some time to overcome, and stress or busyness addictions are no exception. When we go cold turkey, withdrawal symptoms are inevitable. But it's important, because stress has a negative effect on remembering. Constant stress leads to the release of flurries of stress hormones, and these interfere with the processes of memory. *Even at a chemical level*, stress is bad for remembering effectively.

We can't remember, or form memories, as well as we want to – or should be able to – when we're living stressful lives. This alone should make us think hard about our lifestyles. The more we feed the addiction, the harder it is to do without it.[5] How can we ensure we remember God effectively and productively in our lives when we are living in a way that *makes* us forgetful?

Invisible Rulers of Daily Living

What are our priorities? How do we structure each day? If we look at the amount of time we spend doing certain things, and then compare this with what we *say* is most important to us, it can be frightening. I'm always telling myself that my faith in God is the most important thing to me, but is my lifestyle reflecting it? Am I living in a state of remembering, where my faith and my relationship with God are paramount in forming the way I live my life? (This is where I look embarrassed and shuffle my feet.)

I have to face up to the fact: God, for all my lofty words, is not often on my mind. I usually care more about myself than I do about God, or try and mould God in *my* image when in reality I'm made in God's image. I'm distracted, forgetful and frequently disinclined to do anything about it.

This is what happens in the clutter of our lives, when other memory makers crowd in and steal our allegiance. Spiritual amnesia sets in when worry, stress and misplaced priorities crowd into our minds, demand our attention and inhibit our ability to remember.

[5] See Gerald G. May, *Addiction and Grace: Love and Spirituality in the Healing of Addictions* (HarperCollins, 1998), pp. 86–89.

They wrap their stems and hooks around us and slowly begin to throttle us until it becomes so dark we can no longer see the light, or detect its direction. Growth is stunted; we become spiritually malnourished, and we wonder why we feel withered, weary, and lifeless.

Empty Imitations

When this happens, we cannot bear good fruit. At best our lives will be empty imitations. Our responses to difficult situations will betray our deepest secrets: we no longer remember who we are called to be. We no longer trust, because we no longer remember why we should. We have fallen prey to the lure of other memory makers.

Unhelpful memory makers paralyse our effectiveness. The church is full of frozen people who cannot act or react in the way they should or even want, paralysed by the agitation in their minds – Christians choked by the cares of the world, rendered inefficient and miserable because of it.

Western culture tells us that we can rely only on ourselves. When we find ourselves faulty and unsure, we can suffer identity crises which result in breakdown or paralysis. Crises that mean we're looking in the wrong places to 'find ourselves', running around trying meet all the differing expectations that are made of us, dislocated from peace and hope and wondering why we are always so desperately tired.

All the things that press in upon us and clutter our vision demand energy, and lots of it. We stretch ourselves to our limits trying to meet the demands made of us with no back up; we don't know where to find it. We forget that rest is God's invention. We consider time spent with him as something we simply cannot spare. (We would never, of course, say it was a waste of time. We would never *say* that.) We forget that all that we are and all that we are meant to be comes from him. We forget the things that are really important, and tell ourselves we will get to them eventually, that it will happen sometime, when life is more conducive to it. We forget that our strength can only reach so far. We forget that our arms are too short to save.

We forget. We forget. We forget.

Help me God, I'm overloaded.
I've got myself all tangled up
with worry and busyness and stress
and I don't know how to get myself untangled.

Help me.
Help me to see you.
Help me remember.

FOR REFLECTION

- Describe a typical day in your life (if there's no such thing as 'typical', try describing yesterday). Include all sorts of things, be they work, rest or play. Take it further – try and describe the sorts of things you *think* about, what occupies your mind in moments of quiet. Underline the factors you feel are most important. Is there anything missing, something you wish was there? Be as honest as you dare!
- Note the unhelpful elements. How much time do you spend feeling worried or stressed? When is this most likely to happen?

*As my life was ebbing away,
I remembered the LORD;
and my prayer came to you,
into your holy temple.
Those who worship vain idols
forsake their true loyalty.*
Jonah 2:7–8

Chapter 3
A World of Wanting

'Do not store up for yourselves treasures on earth, where moth and rust consume and where thieves break in and steal; but store up for yourselves treasures in heaven, where neither moth nor rust consumes and where thieves do not break in and steal. For where your treasure is, there your heart will be also.'
Matthew 6:19–21

There are other cares of the world that distract us from remembering. Cultural expectations can tease us into believing that if we have *this* or achieve *that*, our lives will be better. Often the first question people ask when we first meet is 'what do you do?', labelling us by our occupation, not by who we truly are. After a while, the two get mixed up in our minds. We are defined only by the job we do, or by the things that we own. We forget the life to which we are called, and replace it with other ideals – money, success, power.

Property and Possession
We pursue the things we want to have, and get depressed when we never reach them. We define ourselves less by the stories of our lives and more by the things of our lives. Our identity and value hinge on our possessions, what we wear, how we appear, what we can do to look good in a world that that values looking good (not the same as *being* good – in the true and beautiful sense of the word). Do we value the right things? Or do they simply add to our forgetfulness – focusing our attention on things we think we want, not the things we need? We put the weight of our deepest needs in places not strong enough to hold them.

In our frenetic world of wanting, we run around chasing the things we think will fulfil all our desires. If only we had the perfect job, gadget, house or partner, we would be satisfied. If only we had enough money to do this or that, we could live healthily and happily. But we can't find exactly what we want, and if we do, it's not as secure as we need it to be. We're made redundant. The mortgage is too high and there are structural problems we had not foreseen. The person we've placed all our hopes in turns out to be – well, only *human*. They hurt us, disappoint us, even leave us. In the end we're exhausted by all this rush for possession and security – disillusioned and depressed. The longing of our hearts is cluttered up by things or goals that offer temporary satisfaction but, eventually, show themselves to be full of holes.

Prosperity: The Quest for Success

Achievement is not a bad thing in and of itself, but when achievement and success define a person's value, problems arise. Unemployment, disability, all the unpredictable circumstances that life throws at us: all this can prevent us from matching up to society's ideal model of success. Couple this with the need for immediate results and instant satisfaction and the problem gets worse. Apparent 'failures' lead to a sense of uselessness.

If we turn achievement and success into mini-gods to which we offer worship, failure – inevitable failure – has the power to undermine us. The irony is that this approach can make us less likely to 'succeed' because we fall into a slump, feeling we can never make something of ourselves. The 'first will be last' kingdom vision of Jesus has a very different slant on success from the stress-fuelled corporate ladder.

There have been points in my own life when 'achievement' has not been easily measurable. Confined by circumstance or poor health, I've watched my friends and peers move into exciting new ventures while I've been left in apparent limbo. It's hard not to cave in to resentment or, at the very least, sadness. But some of the greatest growth occurs during times of waiting.

Our culture doesn't place value on waiting. At least, not a healthy kind of waiting. Often we think we'll be successful if only we did this, or had that. It's true in our lives of faith, too. Somehow we manage to box our ideas of God into what we feel we need in order to progress in faith and maturity. Can God not speak to me in my life now? Is he hampered by my limitation? Is he not the God of the ordinary moments as well as the extraordinary?

We do ourselves a disservice by living in this kind of waiting. We don't bother seeking God now, because we're waiting for a better opportunity (or, perhaps, fewer distractions). We put things on hold until an occasion presents itself – and the months and years bleed away and we never move on from that unhelpful waiting.

Some waiting is helpful. It recognises God within the waiting, informing us, helping us to grow. But the sad limbo of '*I will when*

I get more...' is all too common. I kick myself when I think of times when I believed that life had to have a certain mould in order for me to become who God wanted me to be. I realise now that it was really about me wanting things to be a certain way, but God had different ideas. I wasted time by wishing I was in different circumstances. Don't we all?

The New S Word

With the focus on achievement, ideas of sacrifice have slipped out of our lives. In fact you could say that in many ways, *sacrifice* has become a dirty word. Sacrificial language has become doormat language. This is a world where we have to stand up for ourselves and not let others 'walk all over us'. Turning the other cheek is often perceived as weakness, not strength. Sticking it out for the long haul at great personal cost is not a popular option. We are far more into rights than we are into responsibilities.

We want value. We believe this comes from recognition. We don't want to sit on the sidelines; we're greedy to be *noticed*. Qualifications, awards, trophies, promotions: these are things by which we measure value. The value of what we do in the secret place is underrated (unless, of course, it is cause for scandal or gossip). Often we are so busy focusing on our own visibility (or lack of it) that we forget to notice others. We forget to look at the 'not me' in a world that idolises the 'me'. And we forget the God who sees us as we really are.

One of our greatest fears is that we will be invisible, our lives a mere blip of nothingness on the vast landscape of existence. A results-driven culture only exacerbates this. There's little time allowed for slow growth and maturation. In a world full of eyes, we fear that no one will see us – if they don't see us, they won't value us, and without value we have no sense of purpose or power.

Power and Popularity

> *Am I now seeking human approval, or God's approval? Or am I trying to please people? If I were still pleasing people, I would not be a servant of Christ.*
>
> Galatians 1:10

Even for those of us who do not aspire to position and influence, the lure of power can be – well, powerful! It's so easy to want power on a micro level, even if we don't recognise it.

We can want power in our relationships. We want to prove ourselves right in an argument, to win points even if this means wounding a loved one. We want 'our way or no way'. Sadly, this also happens in churches. Power play in church congregations is an ugly thing. The need to be in control, not allowing for different approaches or different opinions, can damage and destroy. Even if we believe with absolute sincerity that we are right, riding roughshod over others and their opinions does not inspire people to listen to us.

Society leads us to believe that some people's words are more important than others. In a world of soundbites and re-tweets, it becomes a competition to be heard. Is popularity a measure of character? I think most of us would say 'no'. Nevertheless, in a popularity-craving culture, if we feel we're slipping out of view, if others are getting more attention and we're not rated or ranked so highly, we feel put out. Something within us has bought into the idea that how the world measures us is the most important thing.

The Bible envisions a very different attitude. We shouldn't use the world as a measuring rod. In fact, the opposite is true. Getting a bad rating from the world and going *down* in the popularity rankings is inevitable when embracing the upside-down-ness (or perhaps right-way-up-ness) of kingdom living. The legacy of Jesus has frequently caused his followers derision, and worse.

> '*Blessed are you when people revile you and persecute you and utter all kinds of evil against you falsely on my account.*'
>
> Matthew 5:11

There's no adulation, adoration or top-ten attraction here.

The good stuff – the stuff that *would* gain us approval – we're called to do in *secret*, where God sees and God rewards. Human approval, it seems, is a far lesser reward. But how tempting and how addictive human approval can be! How often we take the path of the street-corner hypocrite, wanting our 'holiness' to be seen and acknowledged, longing to be called 'good' and 'gifted'. We share our 'godliness' in our meetings or on social media sites, wanting others to approve and 'like' our updated status, our thought for the day. We think we're sharing Christ, but often we're simply sharing ourselves.

All this desire for human approval nudges out our memories of the God who sees the secret place, who knows exactly who we are, and sees both our bad intentions and our good intentions. It is only God who sees our hearts, and most of us would admit that our motives are muddled and conflicted. Often we desire to be bigger and better, even in our own small world. But it's all gone higgledy-piggledy somewhere, and we are profoundly dissatisfied, recognising that success and popularity are fickle things. If we tie our sense of worth to them, we risk pulling ourselves down with them when they fail us. If our displays are unacknowledged we feel empty, unsuccessful. Our feelings in these moments betray our mixed-up motives.

The Famous One

Celebrity culture tells us we can have 'everything' if we're one of the lucky few. It's becoming an ambition to be famous, regardless of the reason for fame. However, 'everything' gets more and more fragile as we hear of yet another fall from grace, another fractured relationship, another disappointment over the behaviour of our heroes, be they secular or religious.

Only one man proved himself to be utterly reliable and worthy of carrying all our hopes. Jesus showed us what God was like, but he also showed us what we could be like, giving us a glimpse of real humanity. When we encounter the reality of the crucified and risen Christ for ourselves, all the rest proves itself to be merely flimflam. Even Paul, bearing all the marks and qualifications of Judaic faith, counted it all as 'rubbish' compared to knowing Christ.[6]

Jesus outdoes everything and everyone, but so often we ascribe greatness to other inadequate 'stuff'. Our worlds of wanting simply don't compare to Jesus and his outlook on life. Too often we place him at the sidelines of our lives, while we pursue our goals. But he *is* the goal of our lives, isn't he? He's not a cosy feeling, or a comfort blanket, or an intangible philosophy. He's more real than anything we have ever known. But we forget him. We forget how good, how true, how amazing he really is.

The Idols of Our Hearts

Consider your own call, brothers and sisters: not many of you were wise by human standards, not many were powerful, not many were of noble birth. But God chose what is foolish in the world to shame the wise; God chose what is weak in the world to shame the strong; God chose what is low and despised in the world, things that are not, to reduce to nothing things that are...

1 Corinthians 1:26–28

Forgetfulness is not as inactive we may think. Usually, even if unconsciously, the holes in our memories are filled with other things. Other desires, other worldviews, other gods. Our substitute ideals very easily turn to idols. We may not say 'my goal in life is to

[6] Philippians 3:8.

have a wonderful partner, a successful career, the most up-to-date computer/tablet/phone, a nice house and to earn lots of money', but if we buy into the thought that our worth as individuals is based on these things, forgetting the worth given us by God, we become ruled by other lords. We are concerned not with God's approval but with human approval, with human standards instead of God's standards.

Ours is a world where we compete for visibility, especially in the digital spheres of life. Does the sheer variety of digital media available help us or hinder us in our remembering? What would happen if all these facilities and gadgets were taken away, cutting us off from our dizzying array of worlds?

If we hold these things lightly, they do not rule over us. Like so many things, they are tools which can be used well or badly. If they start to be identity formers and informers, absolute essentials to apparent wellbeing, we need to rethink how we see them and how we value them. For it is God's approval that matters, and nothing should take God's place. If something does, it's become an idol, and any helpfulness we derive from it is far outweighed by the harm done by misplaced priority and trust.

God chose the foolish things, the weak things, to shame the wise and the strong. All these things that tug at us, making promises of prestige, popularity, privilege – all the 'P's of the world – are completely different from the life God calls us to live.

And it would be so easy
– wouldn't it? –
if I had the things that others do?
Or maybe it wouldn't.
Creator God,
help me be
who you made me to be
here and now
and seek no applause
but yours.

FOR REFLECTION

- Take stock: note the things you feel you couldn't live without.
- What do you think you need to have in order to mature in faith?
- Whose approval matters to you most? Why?

God is our refuge and strength,
an ever-present help in trouble.
Therefore we will not fear, though the earth give way
and the mountains fall into the heart of the sea,
though its waters roar and foam
and the mountains quake with their surging.
Psalm 46:1–3 (NIV)

Chapter 4
Thieves

*'Come to me, all you that are weary and are carrying heavy
burdens, and I will give you rest. Take my yoke upon you,
and learn from me; for I am gentle and humble in heart, and
you will find rest for your souls.'*
Matthew 11:28–29

Just as there are memory makers in our lives that make us focus
in the wrong place and things that leave us wanting more, there
are things that steal memory. Tiredness and fear are effective co-
workers, each making the other worse and stunting our ability to
follow Jesus wholeheartedly.

Terrorised by Tiredness

Tiredness breeds forgetfulness. Our responses become slow. Our
thoughts slip away easily, dishevelled and disorganised. We long for
a way to recharge.

I'm well aware of the debilitating effects of tiredness, as I have
suffered for many years from Chronic Fatigue Syndrome/ME. At some
points it is manageable and I can adapt life around it. At other times, it is
more severe. Tiredness at this degree is more than a lack of energy. This
tiredness has teeth. It affects more than the physical, impacting mental,
emotional, spiritual and social areas of life. I've discovered that, as an
introvert, confidence itself requires energy, so meeting new people or
even making a phone call when I'm exhausted can be hugely daunting.
I feel dull-witted and drained, unable to think or pray. My eyes strain to
read; lights feel too bright. Frustration leads to sadness at my limitations.
Concentration is harder; suddenly going blank becomes habitual.

When we're tired, we can't think straight. Our power of recall
is weakened from within. Perspective gets out of shape; priorities
are skewed. Issues in life become heavier, problems more acute
and more difficult to resolve. Molehills become mountains. The

important issues get buried in a pile of anxieties and chores. We experience meltdown in our minds and our bodies, struggling to maintain the management of our lives. We become experts at 'coping' with living, keeping our heads above water while straining with our toes to touch the bottom.

We're not particularly good at managing tiredness. Warning signs may be noted, but then dismissed. Worse, we accept it as a normal part of life. 'How are you?' someone may ask. 'Oh, you know,' we reply. 'Tired.' It's a standard refrain in a busy world. Like busyness, tiredness is normal, even expected. There's nothing to be done about it. We confess it, but we don't address it.

Tiredness is a thief. It steals potential. It steals hope. Eventually, it steals time. Overdrawing in the present will always lead to problems in the future.

Overdraft

Often we live in a boom and bust cycle, doing as much as we can while we have energy (the boom), then suffering the consequences later, when we realise we have overdrawn on our resources (the bust). The things that suffer most are those supposedly most important to us: our relationships with family and friends, and our relationship with God. These get neglected and forgotten when we drain ourselves of all spare energy.

As part of managing my illness, I've had to schedule in regular 'rest stops' and manage my levels of activity in order not to become 'overdrawn' on energy. This has not been easy. Lying down when there are things to be done makes me twitchy! It takes discipline to stop when you want to go, to say no when you long to say yes. It's easy to ditch wisdom and go with what we want, and how we feel at the time, regardless of the consequences.

The consequences of overdoing it and expecting too much of ourselves can be very damaging, not just in the short term. We become sluggish, dazed and impotent. Our actions no longer reflect our calling as Christ followers, but our desperate need to stop in a 'go' culture. Our actions do not speak of love, justice and compassion, but of exhaustion, stress and the tension of being constantly over-stretched. By trying to be more effective, we end up becoming less effective.

Church in an Age of Chronic Fatigue

This cycle exists in many lives – in many Christian lives. The demands of the world are increasing. We work hard, we play hard. We often forget to rest hard. We pour ourselves out at work, at home, at church. We try to meet expectations from all corners of our lives, continually giving out, unwilling or unable not to do so. There are things that simply can't *not* be done. We give until we have nothing left. We live out the boom and despair in the bust.

Many Christians willingly give up much time for their church. Some seem to have boundless energy, but others, after years of giving and of doing, feel exhausted and flat. Disillusionment follows as the sense of achievement recedes. Expectations and demands feel heavier, more constricting, less likely to be met.

In a world where success is measured by achievement, rest is rarely seen as constructive. We forget that the original reason for the Sabbath day was rest, pure and simple. We can be tempted to fill our 'spare time' with things we need to do, things we want to do, ways to please others, ways to please God. But in times of regular rest we have an opportunity to encounter God on a much deeper level than when we are running around frantically trying to do things *for* God.

Commonly we mistake distraction for rest, still frantically 'doing' in different ways. 'A change is as good as a rest.' Not necessarily. A change may be good, valid and satisfying. This doesn't make it restful.

Additionally, if poor health or circumstances prevent us from doing things, we can feel disappointed, impotent, useless. If we can change our understanding of rest, we can see it as achieving something in itself, something no activity could achieve.

Lifestyles and habits are not easily changed. To establish a pattern of rest, a pattern of time set aside with God, is a slow and gentle process. Every person has unique aspects to his or her life, but many feel a need for space and rest that is not being met.

Rest Is God's Invention

Do we believe our activity is what gives us worth in God's eyes? In Isaiah 30, God speaks to his people about how they are stubbornly determined to find help in other places. They have looked to Egypt for help instead of their God, carrying out their own plans instead of his. It is in this context God says: 'In repentance and rest is your salvation, in quietness and trust is your strength, but you would have none of it' (30:15, NIV). We often try to find help for ourselves, forgetting to trust in God's way. We buy into the widely accepted ethos of achievement and success, but all our efforts to make, do and achieve are useless in helping us grow closer to God if we do not take time to trust and rest in his presence. Our God wants us to have rest in him, but so often we have none of it.

Rest is essential for remembering. Our memories suffer as our cognitive abilities struggle under the weight of fatigue. They're dominated by recognition of our tiredness. We can't receive or process information properly, so we don't remember things properly. Our 'spiritual' memories suffer as we do not have the time or energy to invest in them, to nurture them, to make them a reality in our everyday lives. Tiredness meddles with our productivity, making us feel awash with failure or even guilt.

Guilt has its own numbing effects: taking our eyes off the goal, sending us into the gloomy back alleys of our lives. It consumes our thoughts and our remembering. We end up asking one of the biggest 'whys' we experience. If my life in Christ is all about being transformed, why isn't it happening? Where is that joy I'm supposed to experience? Why is it all so bland and wearying and empty? Surely I must have missed something? What have I forgotten?

> *I scratch the surface of my mind,*
> *hoping to find some kind*
> *of reaction, of response*
> *of remembering.*
>
> *Astonished at my own weariness*
> *how could I have stretched myself so far*
> *and neglected to recognise*
> *the impact on my heart?*
>
> *Remind me, when the tide rolls in*
> *and I am taken by its force –*
> *remind me then, that in spite*
> *of my exhaustion and my blindness...*
>
> *...you can see me.*

Losing Confidence

Without memory, we feel ill-equipped to tackle things. If I have forgotten how to do something, or never properly learned how to do it, I lack confidence or feel anxious about attempting it.

Memory depends on taking time to receive and store information. When we're hampered in our attempts at doing this, our understanding is patchy. We fill in the gaps with what we think should be there but we're not sure. We plug the holes with platitudes and snatches of things we have heard. They don't feel watertight, but we feel the need to keep them there. We find ourselves getting more and more uncertain. Forgetfulness causes fear.

This can be particularly true when thinking about matters of faith, because these things are close to our hearts and important to us – *they matter*. If the things we believe in suddenly seem tenuous or uncertain, we lose our footing and we feel afraid. Platitudes keep us plodding along on the outside while masking an inward panic at their inadequacy. We need to explore what we believe and why we believe it, otherwise we are left with uncertainty and fear. Fear that none of it was ever real. Fear that people have being lying to us all along. Fear that God is not there and we are unloved and unredeemed, accidental and incidental.

Dancing with Fear

If we have not taken time to reflect on the heart of our believing, we will begin to flounder. Our sense of self depends on what we remember. The reverse is also true – fear makes us forgetful. Like worry, it drowns out everything else with its discordant melody. Like misplaced ambition, it warps our focus to the detriment of everything else. Like tiredness, it drains us and saps us of energy and hope. Another thief of memory, fear is exhausting.

Fear steals even the simplest processes and constricts us, imprisons us. When fear becomes master, memory is stifled. We don't remember past promises, we don't recall hope for the future. We feel only a sense of dread. We try swamping it with trivial, mundane things that prevent us from thinking too much, because we can't cope with facing the black hole opening inside us. It's just *too* black.

Blind Faith?

Sometimes it feels as if faith is *supposed* to have holes in it. That if we know too much, we can't have faith. I'm not convinced that this is the faith we read about in the Bible. That faith is not baseless, without knowledge; it's not unwilling to tackle difficult questions. Faith is not blind; it has amazing vision. That's the point. Faith looks to what is unseen! It can do this because it's built on something sure and certain, a hope given to us by the knowledge of God's glory, something we find in the face of Christ.[7] Love revealed, love conquering, perfect love that drives out fear.[8]

True faith is wise, discerning, knowing – not with passing knowledge but with the wisdom of heaven. There is nothing flimsy about our faith, even if we're clinging to it by a single thread. Yes, sometimes it does involve taking risks, but these risks are based on what we know about the God we follow, rising above our feelings and our anxieties.

Often we settle for flimsy faith. We intend to invest in it, learn and reflect upon it but all the other stuff of our lives crowds in and we lose steam. We neglect our most precious assets and forget about storing treasure in heaven. Our hearts are located in our earthly treasures and securities. We forget that God is our refuge, our strength – that we need not fear because of who *God* is. We get caught up in the things that don't matter, the jots and tittles, the dotting of the 'i's and the crossing of the 't's. Our faith, our confidence and our ability to remember *who we are* get undermined. How can we remember what we have never really grasped?

If we don't know our stories, and have never applied them to our lives or made an effort to understand them, we will find it difficult to understand the importance of a faith that remembers. Our Story – the big, overarching salvation story that threads through history, has always called on us to remember. But even within that Story are tales of our forgetfulness. From these we learn the importance of our remembering, of *why* we should remember, of *how* we remember.

It's God's story. And through his grace, it's also ours.

Lord, keep me from thieves.

FOR REFLECTION

- List the things you find energy-draining in life. Consider: how much does tiredness impact your life and the lives of those around you?
- Did you write a description of a typical day in Chapter 2? Look at it now. How much is given over to rest, without agenda? Is there anything you need to change?
- What are your deepest fears?

[7] 2 Corinthians 4:6.
[8] 1 John 4:18.

I remembered you, God, and I groaned;
I meditated, and my spirit grew faint.
You kept my eyes from closing;
I was too troubled to speak.
I thought about the former days,
the years of long ago;
I remembered my songs in the night.
My heart meditated and my spirit asked:
'Will the Lord reject for ever?'
Psalm 77:3–7 (NIV)

Chapter 5
In a Darkened Room

I am weary with my crying;
my throat is parched.
My eyes grow dim
with waiting for my God.
Psalm 69:3

The ground is hard with frost. Last year's leaves cluster in heavy, swollen lumps. The evenings are dark, spent huddled near a heat source. We become accustomed to wrapping up warm, to half-hearted sunshine, to gloom.

Then one day the sun rises and feels a little warmer; a breeze skips through and with it brings a hint of what was, and what will be again. There's a momentary feeling of the oncoming spring.

It can be startling, this sudden reminder. Reduced to auto-pilot, we feel our way through the current circumstance and forget – no longer *actively* recall – that this is not for ever.

The Blank Screen

When we are wrapped in winter, summer becomes a different reality, another world. When we are surrounded by gloom and darkness, we can forget the warmth of the sun. What if we spent our days in a darkened room for weeks, or even months? After a while, would we forget what light felt like? Would we doubt the accuracy of our memories? Would we tell stories which no longer had the right ending?

There are times when we do battle with darkness in our lives, be it through suffering or tragedy, illness or loss, loneliness or depression. There are times when the screen goes suddenly blank, when God seems silent. When these times stretch onward, seemingly endless, it becomes easier to forget the sound of God's voice, because we simply cannot hear it. Sometimes we deliberately ignore the memory of light; it only makes the darkness harder.

What role can memory play in times such as these? Frequently the writers of the Psalms, expressing their despair and distress, then doggedly go on to remind themselves of the faithfulness of God in the past, when God intervened in other dark moments and of times when God felt *near*. They tell themselves stories of hope. These are stories of redemption, not merely of 'better times'. They are stories of captivity turned to freedom, sadness to joy, of rescue from desperate circumstances.

Let's face it, this kind of storytelling doesn't always come easy. When we're facing long chapters of darkness and other people tell us their stories of light, the contrast can be painful, making us feel even more excluded. Many of the most powerful testimonies are memories of the darkness itself. They are powerful because discovering God amid the darkness is something very raw, very vulnerable. Too often we focus on the fact that the darkness is not going away. We do not recognise that God is not fooled by darkness, nor daunted by night, nor challenged with light-deficiency.

> *If I say, 'Surely the darkness shall cover me,*
> *and the light around me become night',*
> *even the darkness is not dark to you;*
> *the night is as bright as the day,*
> *for darkness is as light to you.*
> Psalm 139:11–12

The kind of forgetting we do in the darkness is that we tend to assume this means that God is not with us. We assume that God will meet us in the same way in which God has always met us. We assume God talks only one language, but our God is multi-lingual and has excellent night vision. We may not be able to hear or see God in ways that we recognise, but God can certainly hear and see us.

God in the Dark

The problem with the darkest moments in life is that they're difficult to address from the outside without sounding clichéd, patronising, or simply ignorant. Aside from the demons of our own mind, only God can address us from inside the darkness. We can't always hear, because sometimes God's presence is silent. Frequently, in my own experiences of darkness, I have expected communication to be active, not passive. I neither understood, nor realised, that I dressed God up too frequently in my image.

In moments of darkness, we need honesty. Often we think we have to conform to a certain template, to sing a certain song – but when things get twisted out of shape or the key changes we are suddenly stumped. We feel we have to hide the fact, to pretend all is still the same. But the darkness will not let us. We are left with the honesty of who we are now and how we feel now. This is a different reality, one which is hard both to confess and to navigate.

Our memories need to adapt, distinguishing surface experience from the deep, unchangeable truths. Sometimes, our memories need correcting. We assume things about people when we do not face what they are facing. Plunged into darkness ourselves, we can only admit and repent of our lack of understanding. New memories are formed in the darkness. They can be painful, but they can also be profound and life-changing in ways that we cannot, in the midst of it, identify. Sometimes we find others in the darkness with us, crying and stretching out their hands to us, if only to cling on grimly (not knowing what else to do).

Sometimes, darkness shows us how gaping the holes in our memories have become. All those temporary, tempting memory makers – worry, ambition, stress – grind to a halt. Without our normal distractions, we are left with ourselves. This can feel quite frightening when we've been so busy filling every moment. We don't know what to make of silence; we are so comfortable with noise. We *talk* about wanting silence and space, but when we find it, it can come as something of a shock. Our makeshift identity markers are stripped away. Who are we? Our very identity feels muddled and raw. We're swamped with feelings of inadequacy, panic and despair.

Depression is a playground of forgetfulness. Memory becomes a cruel contrast between now and then, between me and you. Energy is sapped so that we can't pay attention or retrieve our memories easily. It snatches hope and starves faith. It undermines our memories so that we do not trust past experience and past faith. There is only the darkness, that black hole within.

It takes every ounce of our strength to reach in and find elusive memories, looking for something to give us significance, to give us hope. When the memory makers and the distractions recede – proving how insufficient they really are – we reach out, longing to remember something deeper, something greater, something of *substance*. Something strong enough to last, even in a darkened room.

> *God, in the blanket of my sadness*
> *I feel nothing else –*
> *would you mind*
> *climbing under it with me*
> *just so I know you're there?*
> *I hardly know myself any more,*
> *let alone anything – or anyone – else.*

Seeing Red

The black holes in life express themselves differently from individual to individual. Sometimes we retreat inside ourselves. Sometimes the blackness turns to red and breaks out as rage. Frustration, indignation, stress, hurt and depression all combine with explosive force. Repressed and unresolved anger can become a real problem, and like worry, hampers our remembering by playing out the same old cycles of rage and despair. It rehashes old hurts and repeats old lies: lies about others and lies about ourselves. Everything becomes tinted with it; it's hard to reason with anger at full strength.

Memory retreats as anger takes centre stage. We do not remember previous resolutions of restraint. If we do, they seem unreasonable or unattainable. We dismiss all attempts at comfort; soothing words may even ignite the anger further. It's a force hard to stop. Destruction ensues – of friendships and family relationships, of effectiveness at work, of self-esteem. Anger at oneself is often the hardest to resolve, and has a tendency to fly everywhere, so the underlying cause remains undetected and untreated.

Some anger is simply a natural human reaction, and can be healthy. Anger at injustice is a healthy kind of anger. Jesus got angry. He even upset a table or two! But this kind of indignation is very different from the darkness of deep-seated anger and painful resentment. Anger can itself be a form of depression, a result of it, or even a cause of it.

This kind of anger tinkers with our memories of truth, tainting them with falsehood and making us into people we don't want to be. It sidesteps our identity in Christ and the fruit of the Spirit, aligning itself with the things of 'the flesh' or sinful nature.[9] Unhelpful and hurtful, anger tells a story which if repeated, drowns out the story of who we are made to be.

Nevertheless, God in his grace can meet us in the deepest, angriest darkness. Help *is* there, and even when we stumble and get it all wrong yet again, love and grace are there to pick us up. They help us remember who we *really* are – for our Father has 'rescued us from the power of darkness and transferred us into the kingdom of his beloved Son, in whom we have redemption, the forgiveness of sins' (Colossians 1:13). Whether we struggle with depression or anger or both, neither have dominion in his kingdom.

I've done it again, God –
overreacted, lashed out
in malice and in rage.

It turns inward then –
regret at my behaviour
only seems to make me
crueller, more angry.

I hate what I've become.

Please separate my sense of worth
from all this nastiness
and help me remember you
when all turns red
and I don't know how to fight it.

Change me, divine comforter
as only you can.

A Deeper Darkness

'Can a mother forget the baby at her breast
and have no compassion on the child she has borne?
Though she may forget,
I will not forget you!'
Isaiah 49:15 (NIV)

[9] See Galatians 5:16–26.

Memory loss is terrifying, and we've already begun to see why. It's the backdrop to our sense of identity, forming the pegs on which we hang our sense of self. And some forgetfulness is truly, deeply frightening, a forgetfulness beyond our control, a forgetfulness caused by illness or injury.

Alzheimer's disease and other forms of dementia understandably worry us. We don't want to lose our sense of self; we don't want to change in personality, or worse, in character – that centre of our morality and our beliefs. For those of us for whom faith constitutes a major part of our lives, both these aspects become even more troubling.

Does God leave us in this deeper darkness? Is the identity we once had gone completely? Our fears are not just for ourselves but for our loved ones, whose suffering is as much if not greater. The distress at seeing a partner, parent or friend gradually lose their sense of reality and identity is appalling. The deepest fear we nurse in the secret place of our hearts is that they will forget *us* – forget all our shared stories, forget that they *love* us. Can a mother forget her baby? We're frightened that she can.

When the love of others is naturally so important in supporting us, in making life bearable in the hard times and in sharing joyful times, to have that love taken from us is an awful, heart-wrenching thought. We are not only defined by memory but by our relationships. Dementia threatens to take them both. No wonder we fear it.

But we can invest dementia with the power to steal our identity when it is more complex than that. It's an erratic disease (and comes in different forms) – our loved ones can be lucid one moment, confused the next. Sufferers themselves are aware that they have forgotten or at least do not know something that they should – where are they? How did they get here? Why don't they *know*? They need to be treated with kindness and reassurance, so even if they cannot place the people around them, at the very least they can sense their kindness. This kindness does not come easy – carers and relatives are under continual strain.

We often consign dementia to a box we want, ironically, to forget about. We begin to consider it hopeless. But we believe in a God of hope! This book is not about dementia, nor do I claim any expertise in this area. But I hope that, particularly in the last section, we can at least find tiny grains of possibility that we can use to remind those who suffer in the deeper darkness of forgetting, dealing with what have been described as 'blank windows'.[10] We may not be able to fill in all the blanks, but we can look for touchstones where faith is remembered, and which God in his grace uses to touch us. I suggest that remembering God is a deeper, far less easily boxed kind of remembering – not a single window but permeating the very stones of the building. By forming associations and embracing ways of remembering we can deliberately pepper our lives – and the lives of others – with reminders and flavours of God.

So as we embrace the importance of knowing our stories, we do so acknowledging that God is always gracious, remembering even when we cannot.

Always, he is able
to remember us,
when all our stories have seeped away
when life has fractured
and we struggle to find ourselves
he is able, always
to remember us.

FOR REFLECTION

- What kind of darkness do you – or those you know – most commonly experience? If you have a testimony of darkness, write it down. Note what you felt/are feeling. Make an effort to be honest.
- List some of the things you are afraid of forgetting. Go through them slowly, praying about each one. You may wish to write down your prayers so that you can re-read them at a later time, as an aid to remembering.
- Take a moment to reflect on the fact that God will never forget us.

[10] See, for example, Kate Read, 'What is dementia?', in *Between Remembering and Forgetting: The Spiritual Dimension of Forgetting*, ed. James Woodward (Mowbray, 2010), pp. 2–3.

Part II
An Ancient Dilemma

Chapter 6
A History of Forgetting

Remember the wonderful works he has done,
his miracles, and the judgements he uttered,
O offspring of his servant Israel,
children of Jacob, his chosen ones.
1 Chronicles 16:12–13

Our lives are full of reactions and responses to what we learn and remember. Nevertheless, for all their preciousness, our memories can be selective. Distraction sears through every day, especially in an age where so much information is available to us, compelling us to shift our gaze from one thing to another at an ever-increasing speed. We recognise the importance of remembering, but we are in the habit of forgetting.

This is nothing new.

Turning Back the Years

From the very beginning, humanity has had a history of forgetting. From the stories of our creation to the generation of Noah, from Abraham's journey of faith to Jacob and his sons, from the slavery of Egypt to the Exodus – there are tales of our forgetting. We have forgotten the goodness of our creator; we have forgotten his trustworthiness; we have forgotten his ways.

Abraham, father of many, is remembered for his faithfulness. Yet he was not immune to forgetting God – forgetting to trust him, forgetting the covenant that had been made between them. In the early days of his calling, the then named Abram escaped to Egypt in a time of famine. He pretended his wife was his sister (a half truth, a 'white lie'), to everyone's ultimate displeasure. Pharaoh, the very man he was trying to placate, berated Abram for not telling the truth about the beautiful Sarai and booted him out of Egypt.

According to Genesis this happened not once but twice – once under Pharaoh, latterly with Abimelech, King of Gerar. In spite of God's displeasure and Pharaoh's protest, Abram's concern for his own life made him take the same tack – a tactic he had apparently decided on as soon as they left Haran.[11] But this measure of self-protection put something else in danger – something greater than Sarai's honour.

In doing this, Abram jeopardised the very promise he was called to remember: the promise of offspring borne of Sarai and Abram. If Sarai became a concubine of another man, her children could not be said to be 'Abraham's seed'. In those moments of faithlessness, Abram risked his entire heritage – Israel itself.

Do-it-yourself Promises

Later, in the face of continued failure to conceive, Abram sought a DIY solution at Sarai's own suggestion, by sleeping with Hagar, so that through Sarai's slave girl he may have children and heirs. However, the promise of God had not been a promise of surrogacy. It was the child carried by Sarai who would be the first in line of the numerous descendants promised to Abram, not the child carried by Hagar.

Once again, the divine promise is jeopardised by human actions. Once again, the choices made by Abram and Sarai come back at them, causing pain and regret: Hagar's contempt of Sarai, Sarai's abuse of Hagar, Hagar's escape – returning only at God's behest – and eventual banishment after the birth of Isaac, the child of the promise.

Notably, God did not forget Hagar and Ishmael. It was Hagar who labelled God as the 'God who sees' (Genesis 16.13). God remembered her even when she had been rejected. Even when Abram and Sarai made a mess of things by trying their own way, God did not ignore those who suffered for their mistake but gave them a future of their own.

In Genesis 17 and 18 it is made clear that Sarai was the one by whom the child of blessing will be born; she would be the mother of God's great nation. Both Sarah and Abraham, renamed to reflect their calling and status, reacted with laughter at the possibility. Their laughter of derision became laughter of joy when Isaac was born. Did they forget how amazing their God was? Perhaps they had

[11] See Genesis 20:13.

not yet understood his character and his astonishing power – this God who gave them a child in their old age.

Abraham's Children

What of Abraham's heirs, of Isaac's heirs? Through the muddle and deception of Jacob's story we see that God's people were still grappling with who they were and who God was, still veering between wisdom and foolishness, neglect and favouritism. It was Jacob's favouritism of Joseph that led Joseph's brothers to cast him into a pit, leading to slavery, betrayal, arrest and eventual triumph. Israel, as Jacob was latterly known, moved into Egypt, a land that embraced and honoured the Israelites under the Pharaoh whom Joseph knew, but where Israel grew into so many that the Egyptians complained. When a new Pharaoh ascended the throne, the Israelites became slaves of the very nation that Joseph had once saved from the horrors of starvation. A new hero was needed, a man so reluctant that his brother had to do the talking for him: Moses, to whom God revealed the divine name, YHWH (Yahweh), 'I AM WHO I AM'.

Surely, this was an unforgettable God.

But when Moses finally led the Israelites out of Egypt, a form of chronic forgetfulness made itself known on a large scale. Serious forgetfulness is not merely about being absent-minded. It allows and even chooses that things we have been told slip into disuse, condemned to oblivion or irrelevance.

The ancestors to whom Yahweh had made great promises had birthed a new community needing a sense of identity. This community lived under the umbrella of the previous promise – that they would be blessed and that they would be a blessing. They would be Yahweh's people, and Yahweh would be their God. They needed a framework to live by. Without God's intervention through Moses and the Law, the chosen people would never have had an impact in their world. After all, they started off very badly indeed.

Broken

It was a dramatic event. Moses went up the mountain to receive the law from God – Yahweh, this Lord of lords, who had no other gods before him. The Israelites grew impatient. They thought that *they* had been forgotten, by Moses and this God of their ancestors, made known to them in extravagant ways. They had been born and raised in Egypt, in a climate of deities galore. In the absence of Moses, they decided to build their own god to praise for their escape from Egypt. The Israelites wanted to worship; it was part of their makeup, their culture. Old habits overpowered recent experience. They followed the example of the culture they had previously known. They persuaded Aaron to make the golden calf.

When Moses appeared after having received the Ten Commandments, the Israelites were having an anything-goes party, celebrating their new idol. Moses had been in the presence of the living God. He had known the extraordinary awe and privilege of being spoken to by Yahweh, and then he came down to idolatry at its worst. He reacted with anger – and a dramatic, symbolic gesture. The stone tablets he carried represented the covenant made between God and his people – the essence of the Law, itself a gift, that the Israelites might be Yahweh's people. Israel was unique, chosen, a light to the nations, a shining example, belonging to only one God. Moses threw the tablets down. They were as broken as the people standing before him, having already shattered the precious commandments they'd been given.

Aaron made excuses, but they sounded remarkably like those heard in the garden of Eden – *look what they made me do!* Had Aaron already forgotten the miracles he had witnessed in the escape from Egypt? Was he so willing to attribute this to something crafted from his own hands? The ugliness of idolatry was rarely so acute as in that moment.

Throughout the Old Testament, there is a clear link between 'forgetting' God and transferring worship to other, human-made images. In this clash of real and fake, Moses melted the idol down and ground it into a powder. Then, before he went back up the mountain to get a second set of tablets inscribed with Yahweh's holy law, *he made them drink it.* How helpless, how pointless, was this piece of gold. In the end, it was consumed by the very people who worshipped it. For all the gold, it was worthless. It couldn't save, unlike the One who led them out of Egypt with multiple signs and wonders.[12]

How easily they had chosen to forget.

---

[12] The story of the golden calf is found in Exodus 32.

Past Experience, Present Reality

Looking at the story, we can wonder how those experiencing such dramatic acts of God – be it the plagues of Egypt, the crossing of the Red Sea, or the pillars of cloud and fire in the wilderness – could ever put God out of their minds. Surely, their memories were so fresh, so immediate! Apparently the human tendency to forget goes deeper than matters of proof and experience, deeper than evidence and encounter. We've seen how what we're recalling and thinking about needs to be committed to our long-term memory. Then, it needs to be constantly recalled *back* into working memory in order to impact our current thinking and living.

This is what Israel was called to do, as we'll see in the next chapter. Memory helps define *who we are*. It is essential to our sense of self. So how are God's people defined, and what happens when they forget?

Reading the biblical stories, we are faced with a motley crew of characters. Sometimes they get it right. Sometimes they get it wrong. Sometimes they get it *badly* wrong. When this happens, it often does so because they have forgotten who they were supposed to be. By allowing certain memories to fade, those memories lose their power. Other, less helpful memories and habits of mind are allowed to take control.

We react differently depending on our past experiences. Sometimes this is negative; something dominates us until we cannot see anything except this Thing looming in front of us, warping our view. But the same is true for the positive stuff, except that this informs our current experiences so that we can handle them *better,* not worse. The Israelites in the desert dwelt on the delicious cucumbers of Egypt as they 'forgot' the miserable slavery and all that God had done to free them! Without God's miraculous supply of manna, they would not have had any food in the desert. *In spite* of all his provision, they still doubted his ability to provide for them in the future. They were grumpy. They were stubborn. They were ... human.

So are we.

What Has This Got to Do with Me?

I should say that I personally have not crossed the Red Sea or witnessed a plague of frogs (sorry to disappoint). But I have seen God act decisively in my life, and have forgotten those moments.

I've not ditched the memory altogether but I've neglected to pull it out and dust it down regularly, to re-inspect it, re-invest in it and re-member it. The achingly vibrant reality of it dulls and is lost. If I do think to get it out of its box, I poke dubiously at it and wonder, *did this really happen?* It seems so distant to me now. Far from being a source of faith, it becomes a source of doubt.

Did the Israelites' experience retreat to the back rooms of their minds and not get pulled out again? Did it get swallowed up by new anxieties or older, more stubborn habits? Was it boxed, contained, consigned to irrelevance? Some forgetfulness is deliberate, some accidental. But it is still forgetfulness.

> *How easily*
> *we forget,*
> *disregarding all*
> *we have seen and heard,*
> *all that has been done for us –*
> *so distracted by*
> *our current reality.*
> *Forgive us.*
> *We need to remember.*
> *Remind us who we are.*

FOR REFLECTION

- What strikes you about these Old Testament stories of forgetting? Can you think of other examples?
- What do they tell you about the importance of remembering?
- Can you recall a time when God intervened in your circumstances? What effect did this have on you at the time and does it still affect you now? How?

'Hear, O Israel: the LORD is our God, the LORD alone. You shall love the LORD your God with all your heart, and with all your soul, and with all your might. Keep these words that I am commanding you today in your heart. Recite them to your children and talk about them when you are at home and when you are away, when you lie down and when you rise. Bind them as a sign on your hand, fix them as an emblem on your forehead, and write them on the doorposts of your house and on your gates.'

Deuteronomy 6:4–9

Chapter 7
Commanded to Remember

*'Take care that you do not forget the LORD your God,
by failing to keep his commandments, his ordinances,
and his statutes, which I am commanding you today.'*
Deuteronomy 8:11

Many times in Deuteronomy and elsewhere in the Old Testament, Yahweh, the great I AM, makes remembering a fundamental concern in the Law and commandments. This kind of remembering is more than just possessing a memory of something that has happened.

Memory and Perception
All of us have little pieces of knowledge tucked away in our minds, bits of trivia we've collected. Our brains put filters in place; some things stick, some do not. We have experiences that remain with us and concepts that we form from our knowledge of those moments. When we bring them to mind, we *re-member* them all over again. We rehearse what we already know and as we do so, we form habits of remembering certain things more than others. The more we bring something to mind, the more we continue to remember it.

What is the purpose of remembering? Is it to recall a certain skill, to carry pieces of knowledge around with us until we happen to need them? Memory, we must admit, is more than this. Remembering events, words and the people in our lives forms our sense of identity. Memory gives us markers and milestones – points in our lives and in the lives of others that change us and inform us. *Memory enables us to put into practice what we have learned.*

A 'Doing' Word
The Israelites' memories of Yahweh were memories designed to be *used*, stories to be told and told again: constant reminders of identity. The kind of remembering that Yahweh decrees is an active recall, an attentiveness, something different from simple fact retention. The

meaning of 'remember' in the Old Testament is broader than our ideas of mental recall, or daydreaming about the past. Remembering was a *doing* word, not just a thinking word. (Consider, when people ask God to 'remember mercy' they aren't asking him merely to think about mercy but to be merciful – to *act* with mercy.)

The Israelites set up constant 'memorials' to remind them of events, symbols and stories, to feed memory and hinder forgetfulness. Throughout the people's lives these were constant reminders of God's saving actions in their past.

In Deuteronomy, Moses tells the Israelites: 'Remember the long way that the LORD your God has led you these forty years in the wilderness…' (8:2). Now that they were coming to the end of this particular journey, steps needed to be taken to ensure it wasn't forgotten. They were to remember the unique character and actions of their God. Memory told them where they had come from, told them of their deliverance from Egypt, reminded them that it was God who led them and provided for them. Not only that, it informed how they lived in the present. Their remembering relied on making connections.

Connections keep memories strong and fresh, giving them staying power. This kind of remembering is an active state, working on the principle that we are natural forgetters. Without the *practice* of remembering, people get rusty. Just as a piece of trivia we've bundled away can eventually be forgotten, so we can forget the most important, profound things of all. We forget who we are and how we should live.

The Israelites' identity was bound up in One Person Only – Yahweh, the great I AM. They were a chosen people, God's treasured possession. It was Yahweh who called them, who led them out of Egypt and into the wilderness with pillars of flame and cloud. Their God kept the promises made to their ancestors, for God keeps his promises. They, too, were told not to forget. Their memories of their God would give them confidence in him. Beyond this, if they forgot Yahweh, in a sense they forgot themselves. Their purpose would fracture; their identity would waver. They would become indistinct from all the other nations.

A Framework for Living

Memory is a link between past and present, as well as informing the future. It points to specific events, times and people. For ancient Israel, once the original witnesses of an event had died, it was important that the story was still told in order for its significance to continue impacting the lives of others. Later generations of the Israelites would not have immediate memories of exodus and wilderness. They depended on the collective memory of the people, not just a temporary, individual remembering which ceased when a person died. No, this was a memory that was tied up in their *group* identity.

In our individualised culture, we can miss this significance. But think of participants in family history programmes, such as the BBC's *Who Do You Think You Are?* People are visibly moved on discovering something about their great, great grandparents that they had never realised. They are proud or distressed by their heritage. Learning where we come from still has an impact on us, even in an individual-centred culture like ours.

It was important the Israelites didn't forget where they had come from, because these experiences told them that they were a chosen people, a *rescued* people. In a sense, it allowed them to participate in the previous events – giving them ownership of old memories, even though they had not experienced the original event themselves. They remembered their stories by re-enacting them – in their festivals and special days, in what they ate and wore, in what they sung. In this way, later generations participated in the events of the past, owning the story for themselves. They became new witnesses to an old story. Yahweh was not just the God of their ancestors but their God, too.

Memory provided a framework for living, guiding attitudes and behaviour. It told them to be merciful to the slaves and strangers among them, because they had once been slaves and strangers. Memory pointed them to the source of their blessing. When they entered a land full of plenty, it was not down to them but down to the provision of their God and rescuer. They were not to become blasé about all that they had been given. The book of Deuteronomy itself acts as one huge recap – a great reminder to the Israelites of all they had been given, where they had come from, what they had suffered and what happened when they forgot their God and went after other things.

Mirroring God

Memory and faithfulness have a symbiotic relationship in the commands of the Torah. It's an important connection, and one of the ways in which remembering is a *doing* word. Biblically, forgetting God was associated with pursuing *other* gods, with idolatry – placing something or someone else in the place reserved for Yahweh. By changing the focus of their worship, Israel was not 'remembering' the God of her ancestors but abandoning him, replacing the one true God – as if they really could! – with other things. Faithlessness was seen as forgetfulness.

The effect of this is detrimental to the people. They become what they worship, as the Psalmist proclaims:

> *Their idols are silver and gold,*
> *the work of human hands.*
> *They have mouths, but do not speak;*
> *eyes, but do not see.*
> *They have ears, but do not hear;*
> *noses, but do not smell.*
> *They have hands, but do not feel;*
> *feet, but do not walk;*
> *they make no sound in their throats.*
> *Those who make them are like them;*
> *so are all who trust in them.*
> Psalm 115:4–8

We mirror what we worship. Idols cannot hear, speak or see. We become as deaf, mute and blind as they are. In Scripture, the relationship between people and their allotted 'gods' is dynamic. A kind of reflection takes place. Gods of our own making are formed in our image, a very different thing from our being made in God's image. With the Israelites' decreed worship of Yahweh, this reflection between god and worshipper is shown in radiant lifestyles, markedly different from surrounding cultures. Forgetting God is no mere switching flags or changing stripes. It affects everything. It *should* affect everything. Memory is a hallmark of faith.

For the people of Israel, forgetting God meant that they no longer fulfilled their calling to be a light to the nations, because they neglected the true source of that light. Forgetting God meant curse instead of blessing, bad instead of good. Forgetting God undermined their understanding and their ability to be truly human. This kind of memory loss was fatal.

Kings, Calling and Consequence

Acknowledging forgetfulness can be painful. During the reign of King Josiah of Judah, one of the 'good' kings who was said to do what was right in Yahweh's sight, the High Priest Hilkiah discovered a misplaced and neglected book of the Law in the temple. He passed it to the secretary, Shaphan, who carried it to Josiah and read to the King from the book. Josiah 'tore his robes', for he only then understood the forgetfulness of his people. The people had stopped paying attention to their stories; eventually ceasing to remember them altogether. The words of the Law came as a surprise to Josiah, and his reaction was swift.

He removed all symbols of idol worship from the temple of Yahweh and even desecrated the High Places – where the people had erected altars to other gods – with a thoroughness unique among all the kings that had come before him. Renewing the covenant and pledging to follow Yahweh, Josiah called for a celebration of Passover – that great act of participatory remembering whereby Judah's identity was re-established as a people delivered, by Yahweh, from slavery.

We are told that before Josiah 'there was no king like him, who turned to the LORD with all his heart, with all his soul, and with all his might, according to all the law of Moses; nor did any like him arise after him' (2 Kings 23:25). Through the words of the Law, Josiah remembered on behalf of the people, and acted upon that memory. Because of this, *he* is remembered in scripture – as a shining exception to a general rule.

Josiah came after a plethora of forgetful kings, and the dividing of the Northern and Southern Kingdoms. His actions could not erase the guilt of the people, and the blood shed by previous evil kings, none more so than Manasseh, Josiah's grandfather, who 'filled Jerusalem from one end to another' with innocent blood (2 Kings 21:16). To remember their God meant to keep God's commandments and to follow God's ways, reflecting his character to the wider world. The dirty deeds of the other kings muddied this reflection and gave Yahweh – the awesome, Holy God of their ancestors – a bad name.

The story these kings told was a false story, not reflecting the truth of their Maker and Saviour, not acknowledging their God's character or his saving acts. Kings were seen as God's representatives to the people (and vice versa), but instead they had turned to other gods and led the people astray. The holy calling of kingship was in tatters.

The prophets of Israel and Judah had spoken out against forgetfulness, calling the people to remember Yahweh and his ways of justice and mercy. Nonetheless, like so many of their ancestors, Josiah's sons once again reverted to the old patterns of unfaithfulness. The damage of this forgetfulness, this unfaithfulness, is irreparable. We read in 2 Chronicles:

> The LORD, the God of their ancestors, sent persistently to them by his messengers, because he had compassion on his people and on his dwelling place; but they kept mocking the messengers of God, despising his words, and scoffing at his prophets, until the wrath of the LORD against his people became so great that there was no remedy.
>
> 2 Chronicles 36:15–16

Jerusalem fell. The earthly Zion was ransacked and invaded, the signs of her identity carried away by her enemies. The words in these verses are like stones, cold and hard, a mass of 'if only' moments, each stinging harder than the last. The final phrase gets right under the skin: 'there was no remedy'.

They had forgotten God, and the result was terrible. It had led to all kinds of atrocities, made a mockery of his name and torn their identity into shreds. The prophets had been ignored, the kings had done evil in the sight of God and now those things that made them unique were taken from them: the land, the city, the temple itself – the very reminders they had been given to help them remember! How could they recover from this? Not by their own powers of remembering. It was God who would do the remembering, God who would intervene. For in spite of all they had done, God did not forget them.

> O Lord, in our arrogance we may think
> we are much more civilised
> than this ancient culture –
> but still we have forgotten you
> and in doing so
> have reduced your reputation
> to a sullied version

> *of what it should be.*
> *Look at what we have done –*
> *or neglected to do –*
> *in your name!*
> *Have mercy on us, we pray.*

FOR REFLECTION

- Read the story of Josiah in 2 Kings 22 and 23. Write a description of his character based on what you know of his actions.
- Define 'forgetfulness'. How is your definition similar to or different from the biblical concept of being unfaithful?

By the rivers of Babylon –
there we sat down and there we wept
when we remembered Zion.
On the willows there we hung up our harps.
For there our captors asked us for songs,
and our tormentors asked for mirth, saying:
'Sing us one of the songs of Zion!'

How could we sing the LORD's song in a foreign land?
If I forget you, O Jerusalem, let my right hand wither!
Let my tongue cling to the roof of my mouth,
if I do not remember you,
if I do not set Jerusalem above my highest joy.
Psalm 137:1–6

Chapter 8
Memory in Exile

Jerusalem remembers,
in the days of her affliction and wandering,
all the precious things
that were hers in days of old.
Lamentations 1:7a

When all that we hold dear is stripped away, memory is what remains. When Judah was swept into exile, broken and scattered, it stole her sense of self.

Recurring Rage

Psalm 137 isn't just a lament. It ends in a tirade of bitterness: 'O daughter Babylon, you devastator!' spits the Psalmist. 'Happy are those who pay you back for what you have done to us! Happy shall they be who take your little ones and dash them against the rock!'(vv. 8–9). These verses are among the most uncomfortable in the Old Testament. They are so vindictive and visual, as if the Psalmist is picturing it happening. Are these words fuelled by memory?

This is a human lament for a very human grief, a wail of suppressed rage bursting out and expressing itself in a way that makes us shuffle our feet in embarrassment and horror. *This is how I feel*, says the Psalmist, *see how you would like it, if it was done to you*. It's raw and awkward and appalling. It's humanity stretched to its limit.

The destruction of Jerusalem was merciless. The Chaldeans had no pity on young or old. The 'youths' were killed 'with the sword in the house of their sanctuary' (2 Chronicles 36:17). The safe place had become a murder scene. The walls of the city were broken down; the house of God was burned. Now, in the land of their captors, those left alive are asked to *sing*? How dare their conquerors ask such a thing!

Within the anger of the Psalmist – within the seeping wounds of memory – lies a resolution. *I will not forget.* Memory was horribly painful, but it was essential if the exiles were going to keep hold of their identity.

It was easy to cling to hope offered by false prophets, who kept saying this situation would soon be over. The prophet Hananiah said that the yoke of Nebuchadnezzar would be broken in two years.[13] Yahweh told Jeremiah differently. Only after 70 years would they be brought back to their land.

Life in Limbo

The number 70 often signifies completion. Only after the fullness of the allotted time would Judah be able to return. In the meantime, the people were to settle where they were, building houses and planting gardens, marrying and having children, re-building themselves in this foreign land. This must have been hard for those who cradled the same painful memories as the writer of Psalm 137. Only after 70 years would they call upon Yahweh and would he hear them. Then, Yahweh would allow himself to be found – the God who had plans for them, plans for good and not harm, to give them future and hope.[14] For now, they had to settle where they were.

During this time of waiting, what would sustain them? What would keep them from being completely absorbed into a different culture, an identity far from the Israel of old? They were without land and temple. What they did have was memory, and exile intensified the need for remembering. It was a time for collecting and collating old stories, for examining where they had come from.

The God of Every Place

It's a difficult balance. How did they navigate life in a way that remembered where they have come from and why they were here, while still living in the present? How did they untie their processes of remembering from the land and the temple and fix them instead to a God who is Lord of the whole earth and not just the localised Lord of the Promised Land? They were called to remember past experiences and promises of Yahweh but also to live here and now. Many of them would not live to see the return to Jerusalem (and some would not *want* to return).

[13] See Jeremiah 28.
[14] Jeremiah 29:11.

It was important that the people didn't forget, but if they lived their lives hampered by a kind of absenteeism caused by obsessive nostalgia, they wouldn't be honouring their God. They were to live in remembrance of what has gone before but also to hope, looking towards future restoration.

The temptation to focus on what we used to have can be very powerful. It's a temptation the Israelites faced in the desert, gazing back at rose-tinted Egypt. Now the temptation was even more immense, for these were their memories of the Promised Land. However, nostalgia over possession and status is not the kind of remembering they were called to. It was their *God* who they were to remember, and they needed to adapt their understandings of God. Yahweh was not some local god but was their God wherever they were, even in the place of exile.

Memory is a thread to which faith clings when it is too dark to see. For the exiles of Judah, if the rust of forgetfulness set in now, the ship of their identity would sink. There would be no more remembering, no true return from exile. Eventually nobody would even know that something important had been lost.

Centres of Remembering

The identity of the people was fuelled by reminders of the land (promised to Abraham), the Law (given through Moses) and the temple (the location of the holy of holies, where God's glory was revealed).

The temple had huge significance for Israel, ever since the first 'house of God' was built by David's son, Solomon. It was a place of permanence and presence. In Israel's desert wanderings the tabernacle – the God-tent – had moved with them and before them. Solomon's temple was set in stone, no longer mobile but a fixed point for the people of Yahweh. At the official opening ceremony Solomon prayed:

> *'Hear the plea of your servant and of your people Israel **when they pray toward this place**; O hear in heaven your dwelling-place; heed and forgive.'*
>
> 1 Kings 8:30 (emphasis mine)

Solomon goes on to list various circumstances and situations the people may find themselves in, and asks constantly for Yahweh's response to those who 'pray towards' or 'stretch out their hands towards this place'. The temple was the focus of the prayers of Israel and for the prayers of foreigners who had heard of Yahweh and wanted to find him for themselves.[15] It was a conduit between God and humankind. Here the people directed their petitions, here they laid their present and future hopes. It was a centre of *remembering*. Yahweh responds:

> '*I have heard your prayer and your plea, which you made before me; I have consecrated this house that you have built, and put my name there for ever; my eyes and heart will be there for all time.*'

1 Kings 9:3

Even as he makes this promise Yahweh issues a warning: if Israel turns aside from following him, forgets and abandons him for other gods, he will cut them off from their precious land and 'the house I have consecrated for my name I will cast out of my sight' (9:7). Those who see the ruined house will wonder: why has their God done this to them? The answer: because they have forsaken him and followed other gods. Because they have forgotten.

God of the Past, Present and Future

Judah's forgetfulness, like the other Israelite tribes before her, resulted in her exile. When her active remembering ceased and all her uniqueness was gone, when she repeated the unspeakable acts committed by the land's former inhabitants, there were consequences. The markers of memory, the old identity tags, were removed. Temple and land – a land stamped with memorials and reminders – were taken away. Judah's forgetfulness and faithlessness became her downfall.

The stories of God's previous redemptive acts became desperately important in the 'strange land' of Judah's exile. They needed constant retelling in order to reassure her of the unfailing, unchanging character of God. It was not Judah's track record she needed to focus on to get through exile – it was God's. God the great maker and rescuer had birthed a people from impossible circumstances (Sarah's empty womb) and later delivered his people from an oppressive nation (Egypt, land of slavery). God could do so again.

[15] See 1 Kings 8:41–43.

Now was the time to re-learn old lessons, retrieve old stories and reflect on what this meant for them in their place of exile. God's faithfulness was the one thing they could rely on – so that in the midst of their misery, we hear the cry: 'Great is your faithfulness!' (Lamentations 3:23).

Memory in Mourning

Memory can bring crippling grief, not just because of painful memories but in reaction to the positive ones. We mourn because we remember a time when things were different, and we long for that time again. We wish things were as they once had been.

What do we remember? It's a good question to ask when we are grieving for former times. Do we focus on what God has done for us in the past and celebrate it, sustained by the knowledge that he has delivered us and will deliver us again? Or do we succumb to the temptation of thinking 'we had it so good' and neglect to live in the now, constantly jaded by the difference in our circumstances?

On what – or who – do our memories focus? When circumstances are appalling, good memories can sharpen our agony. We have to choose which memories inform our minds and lives. For exiled Judah, these were the stories of past redemptive acts, times when startling light broke through insistent darkness.

Returning from Exile

> *Is Ephraim my dear son?*
> *Is he the child I delight in?*
> *As often as I speak against him,*
> *I still remember him.*
> *Therefore I am deeply moved for him;*
> *I will surely have mercy on him,*
> *says the LORD.*
> Jeremiah 31:20

As the 70 years drew to a close, the Persian kingdom rose into the foreground. It was the Persian king Cyrus, stirred up by the Spirit of Israel's God, who declared that the temple at Jerusalem should be rebuilt.[16] Those who were willing returned to their homeland, a staggered return of a remnant. Despite opposition, hiccups and

[16] 2 Chronicles 36:23.

delays, the temple was finally rebuilt, and was dedicated as the house of God.[17]

Nehemiah, cupbearer to King Artaxerxes, heard of the still broken-down walls of Jerusalem and was deeply grieved. After prayerful preparation, Nehemiah went to Jerusalem with great fanfare to rebuild the walls. In the midst of opposition from his critics and depression overwhelming the workers, Nehemiah reacted with prayer and positive action. When the people were disillusioned and frightened he said, 'Do not be afraid.' Was it an empty phrase? A mantra, a way of pulling themselves together? No. It was based on one very important thing: the character of their God. Nehemiah appealed to their *memories*. Remember Yahweh, he told them, who is great and awesome. For that reason you have the strength to fight for your kindred, your families and your homes.[18]

God's people are characterised by the very fact that they are God's people. This is why they are rebuilding Jerusalem's walls. Nehemiah's response is prayerful, practical and above all pointed towards the one whose name they know: a great name, a healing name, a name that can change everything.

Remembering works both ways. If our remembering of God is to be active, then God's remembering of us is also active. When God is said to 'remember' his people, it means that God has done something. It's remembering with *direction*. When God remembers, God acts.

As Nehemiah oversees the rebuilding of the walls, he continually asks Yahweh to 'remember' him, requesting that the good deeds of Nehemiah would be credited to God's own memory bank. Nehemiah is committed to the task of rebuilding and restoring that which had been lost, but his frequent plea is that Yahweh himself would take note, be attentive to what has been done, and act toward him accordingly. Nehemiah's last recorded words are deeply personal: 'Remember me, O my God, for good!' (Nehemiah 13:31).

Faithful memory is two-directional; for God not only calls us to remember him, but promises to remember us.

---

[17] See Ezra chapters 3–6.
[18] Nehemiah 4:14.

Remember me, O God
when all is dark
and I can't recall
how I arrived here

Remember me, O God
when all my building
seems fruitless, and others
mock my attempts

Remember me, O God
in places of exile
when it seems that this
may go on forever

Remember me, O God
and help me remember you.

FOR REFLECTION

- What feelings might you experience, if the most important things of your life were stripped away from you?
- Try writing your own prayer, psalm or reflection describing a time of crisis in your own life, or in the lives of those you care about.

Remember these things, O Jacob,
and Israel, for you are my servant;
I formed you, you are my servant;
O Israel, you will not be forgotten by me.
I have swept away your transgressions like a cloud,
and your sins like mist;
return to me, for I have redeemed you.
Isaiah 44:21–22

Chapter 9
The God Who Remembered

And the Word became flesh and lived among us, and we have seen his glory, as of a father's only son, full of grace and truth ... It is God the only Son, who is close to the Father's heart, who has made him known.
John 1:14, 18

The world of the Old Covenant is drawing to a close; the New is ready to begin. This is not a destruction of the old but a fulfilment of it. Light is about to break in, a Light shining more brightly than all previous histories and former heroes. God is about to make himself known in an extraordinary way.

By New Testament times, many Jews felt they were still in exile, in spite of being in their own land. The fall and rise of empires had simply given them a new master. Rome. Although the Jewish nation was given a fair amount of autonomy in religious matters, they did not feel truly free. They longed for Yahweh to remember them, to speak to them again. But when God finally entered the neighbourhood, he was not recognised.

God of the Forgotten

For a child has been born for us,
a son given to us;
authority rests upon his shoulders;
and he is named
Wonderful Counsellor, Mighty God,
Everlasting Father, Prince of Peace.
Isaiah 9:6

When Jesus of Nazareth arrived on the scene, he started small. He was born a fragile baby who, like all of us, needed his head supported until his neck was strong enough to lift it, who wailed at the frightening confusion of the world, who felt the anxiety of hunger, fear, pain and tiredness. When God remembers his promises, he does so in unique ways.

This child was more than anyone expected. In the story of visiting Magi from the East, Matthew tells us they brought with them gifts of gold, frankincense and myrrh – kingly gifts for a child cradled in a manger with no throne in sight.[19] Gold – of great value; frankincense, used in worship; myrrh, used, among other things, to anoint the dead. This child would be so many things: king and priest, prophet and teacher, Messiah and more. What this child would declare about himself would shake the entire establishment. He would come among them and live his life to remind them of God and his ways. In the end, he would give his life. It was the ultimate act of remembering.

Jesus lived the story of the God who remembered. He would point out the things the people had forgotten; he would tell them of a God who did not forget. He hung out with those forgotten by society and dismissed by the authorities, with those who were rarely called to mind, and if they were, only to be condemned. He invited outcasts to re-form their identities around him, to walk after him, to learn from him. He remembered them, when no one else wanted to.

The Director's Cut

Jesus said to her, 'Everyone who drinks of this water will be thirsty again, but those who drink of the water that I will give them will never be thirsty. The water that I will give will become in them a spring of water gushing up to eternal life.'

John 4:13–14

In the account of John 4, as Jesus wearily sits down at Jacob's well, his encounter with the Samaritan woman exemplifies his kind of remembering. By most people she is excluded, ignored, deliberately 'forgotten'. Even in the gospel story she is without name. We know her only by her nationality, her gender and her colourful history. We also know her because she encountered Jesus. That changes everything.

The woman at the well has her own memories and her own understanding of God's story. Jesus takes her memory and infuses

[19] Matthew 2:1–12.

it with previously unseen material, adding a new chapter where God remembers *her* – a Samaritan! A woman! A 'sinner'! This is the director's cut of God's story, the way it was intended to be. A time is coming (and is now here!) when worship will not be confined to one place, when old distinctions will disappear and none will be excluded from the possibility of worshipping the Father. Worshippers will worship in 'spirit and truth'(4:23) and be defined by these things, not by location or nationality. This woman knows that the Messiah is coming; she knows he will explain everything. This is what her memory tells her – her memory of the Big Story and the Big Promises contained within it.

Now Jesus declares *himself* to be the Messiah, the one who will explain everything. He is the One who makes sense of the memories held of the Big Story. God remembered his people in a way they did not expect, and pulled together all the threads of the story into one person: the person of Jesus Christ. This is the person who is before all things and in whom all things hold together.[20] The incarnation of the Son, God-with-us, was something new and yet intended from the beginning. A whole new section of salvation history is launched, but Jesus has always been interwoven through every part, even if he has only been glimpsed through a veil of former things. Now, the Son is made known – even to those whose memories were seen by the religious authorities as dysfunctional or lacking.

The Forgetters

> When the scribes of the Pharisees saw that he was eating with sinners and tax-collectors, they said to his disciples, 'Why does he eat with tax-collectors and sinners?' When Jesus heard this, he said to them, 'Those who are well have no need of a physician, but those who are sick; I have come to call not the righteous but sinners.'

Mark 2:16–17

Jesus' choice of companions was unexpected and frequently disapproved of by those who considered themselves moral and spiritual leaders. The disciples he chose were not religious students but fishermen and tax collectors. They did not go to him and request to be taught, offering their credentials for followership. No, Jesus chose *them*. He didn't seek out a select group of Pharisees

[20] Colossians 1:17.

or synagogue leaders, but went to those overlooked by the establishment.

More than this, he went to those who were despised. He called on tax collectors, often dishonest and seen as Roman collaborators, and reached out to prostitutes. He touched the dead and the dying; he did not shy from those deemed 'unclean'. In fact, far from making himself unclean, he made *them* clean. Everything was upside down. Those who expected to be remembered first suddenly found themselves tagging along, feeling insulted, at the rear. In Jesus' parables they were cast in unforgiving roles, shown up as neglecting God's people and being so concerned with minor details that they forgot that their God was Yahweh, champion of the orphan and widow. Their God was the God of justice, but by puffing themselves up and making themselves look important they neglected to do the most important things.

Shalom

... by his bruises we are healed.
Isaiah 53:5b

When a woman who had been bleeding for 12 years clutched at the hem of Jesus' cloak, she should by law have made *him* unclean. In the moment of her healing, followed by Jesus' affirmation of it, more was done for her than the simple stopping of blood. He restored her to her community.

In her desperation, she had reached out and touched him, probably hoping he wouldn't notice. But of course he noticed. She would not be so easily ignored, so conveniently forgotten. By calling her out in front of the crowd, he reinstated her, and gave her the wholeness and the peace she had lacked for so long. This was no longer a secretive act but a public affirmation.[21]

Jesus' message was one of a God who remembers – a God who cares deeply enough to rip open his heart for his people. The people would never be able to mend the broken bridge, to re-align themselves with their God, to discover their true identity. Without a profound, Spirit-filled relationship with God, they would not be whole. This wholeness did not come cheap. It required someone to be utterly broken. Ultimately, God in Jesus chose the cross.

[21] Mark 5:25–34. This incident is also recorded in Matthew 9:20–22 and Luke 8:43–48.

Cross and Curse

> *Christ redeemed us from the curse of the law by becoming a curse for us – for it is written, 'Cursed is everyone who hangs on a tree.'*

Galatians 3:13

The cross is a symbol of the God who remembers: the personal act of Yahweh, not just turning his attention towards his people and hearing their cries, but getting down and dirty, dealing with suffering and death side by side with those he chose to save. God chose to offer us new hope, a new way of living. *Come, follow me,* said Jesus. He not only calls fishermen and tax collectors. He calls us. He wants to give us back our memories, reminding us that we are formed in God's likeness, made so that we can relate to him. Jesus was and is the ultimate reminder of how much worth God has placed on us, how much love God has for us, how much God is prepared to do in order to help us remember.

God's children had not been forgotten. The way out of exile was not the overthrow of the Romans, their collaborators and everything that smacked of oppression, conquerors and compromise. It was not the toppling of Caesar or the raising of an army. It was a man bleeding on a cross. Under their own law the one who hung on a tree was cursed. There was no such thing as a crucified messiah. Or was there?

If it had ended there, they would have been right. He might still have been called a good man, a perceptive teacher, perhaps even another rejected and persecuted prophet, by some. But he could not have been anointed and favoured by God if the end of his story was crucifixion. Crucifixion meant curse, a sign of God's displeasure.

But death could not hold him. By his resurrection Jesus was vindicated in all he said and did. The 'curse' of the cross simply could not hold; it was shattered. The Law was superseded. Jesus was proven King over death itself. God remembered us in Christ and, through his brokenness, death was broken on our behalf. Suddenly Yahweh's people would find all their identity in Jesus Christ – the new temple, the new Moses, the new Israel. He fulfilled the old markers of temple, law and land in new and startling ways. Now, we are to remember *him*.

Humanity's history may have been one of forgetfulness, but for God it was one of remembering. There is only one kind of forgetting practised by God – the practice of forgetting our sins. He chooses *not* to remember those things that have driven a wedge between us. By the cross he chose to get rid of those things and wipe them from our lives and from his mind.

As the grieving women met the risen Jesus in the early morning of resurrection day, they discovered they had not been forgotten. They were not abandoned. No, God had remembered them, in an act that changed the course of history.

Glory Walk

in the dim light of dawning
in the morning, in the garden
you walked
in glory,
your story not ended,
as was thought, but
the beginning of all our stories –

your body, broken
but now restored
to something far more
wonderful – a taste of
our own risen-ness

master of our hearts
conqueror of death
giver of divine breath,
you walk
in glory

FOR REFLECTION
- Think about times you have encountered Jesus and the wonder of his story. Practise the art of remembering by writing down a description or a list of key words/phrases, or by drawing a picture.
- How do Jesus' words and actions challenge us today? How can we be more like him?
- Take a moment to reflect on what Jesus' death and resurrection mean for us and for our world.

According to Thy gracious word,
In meek humility,
This will I do, my dying Lord,
I will remember Thee.

Thy body, broken for my sake,
My bread from heaven shall be;
Thy cup of blessing I will take,
And thus remember Thee.

Can I Gethsemane forget?
Or there Thy conflict see,
Thine agony and bloody sweat,
And not remember Thee?

When to the cross I turn mine eyes
And rest on Calvary,
O Lamb of God, my sacrifice,
I must remember Thee.

Remember Thee and all Thy pains
And all Thy love to me;
Yea, while a breath, a pulse remains,
I will remember Thee.

And when these failing lips grow dumb
And mind and memory flee,
When Thou shalt in Thy kingdom come,
Jesus, remember me.

James Montgomery (1771–1854)

Chapter 10
The Power of Recall

You shall know that I am in the midst of Israel,
and that I, the LORD, am your God and there is no other.
And my people shall never again be put to shame.
Then afterwards I will pour out my spirit on all flesh;
your sons and your daughters shall prophesy,
your old men shall dream dreams,
and your young men shall see visions.
Joel 2:27–28

One of the most powerful ways we have of remembering the story of our faith is that meal where Jesus said, 'Do this in remembrance of me'.[22] Jesus grounds our remembering of him in a physical act: engaging our senses, thoughts, words, and involving social interaction. We enact and inhabit this striking picture.

Jesus grounded this call to remember in action. Not only that, but he used an act of remembering that the Jews already practised – that of *Passover*. On that terrible night in Egypt, the angel of Yahweh 'passed over' the blood-daubed doorposts of the Israelites, protecting them from the deadly fate of Egypt's firstborn.

The Passover meal was eaten in a hurry, to recall the Israelites' hasty dash from Egypt after that terrifying night was over. A series of questions and answers, from different members of the family, ensured the meaning remained.[23] Their deliverance came at a high price for the Egyptians. Who can suppress a shudder at this story of death stalking Egypt in the darkness?

The Passover was a vivid memorial of a vivid event: the Israelites' departure from their oppressive masters, the conqueror

[22] See Luke 22:14–20. Matthew and Mark record the event of the Last Supper, but not the command to 'remember' Jesus in this way. See also 1 Corinthians 11:23–26.
[23] See Exodus 12, in particular vv. 24–27.

and the conquered switching places, the drama of the exodus. It was a reminder not of slavery in Egypt but of *deliverance* from that slavery. It was one of Israel's most powerful stories, passed down, interpreted and reflected upon from generation to generation.

Now Jesus, Yahweh's own firstborn son, creates something new out of the old. Out of the symbolism of Passover he draws a new covenant: his life, his blood, his saving actions, his death. His task was not to free a nation from another nation, but to offer the chance of freedom for *all* nations. His blood would become the figurative mark on the doorpost, his own self the lamb that was slaughtered. A mission so all-encompassing and so terrifying that it took on the fabric of the universe, the finality of death, and the sin of the entire world. Jesus took an old story and made it new – and far, far bigger.

'Sin', for all its commonness, is not an easy concept to define. Nor is it a fashionable word. Most definitions fall short or shove it into one inadequate mould, using it as a word weapon or confining it to specific actions. I would suggest that 'sin' is a concept that draws together all that separates us from God, all our selfishness, all the darkness in our being, in our world and in our communities. Can we look at the world around us, or our hearts within us, and say that this darkness is not present? That we don't have ways of acting that are damaging, abusive and wrong?

Just as Egypt enslaved the Israelites, so sin enslaves us. Just as the blood of a lamb saved them, the blood of the Lamb saves us. These concepts and images can feel alien to us. Digging into the background to our faith can help. By studying and examining the scriptures and seeking to understand context and meaning, we can try to wear scriptural shoes for a while – taking off our culture's footwear and trying to see how *they* walked. Our feet aren't used to it. These other shoes chafe, rubbing painfully at our feet sometimes. Regardless, it's a valuable and often necessary exercise.

Our memories need shaking up. Words are not enough. The concepts we encounter in our communions, our masses, our memorials – however we celebrate them – commemorate a shocking event. When we set our minds to it, it is the ultimate antidote to the sterilisation of memory. With the help of the Holy Spirit, we repeat and embed the experience, taking the act of remembering into our very selves.

Bearing Witness

> *For all who are led by the Spirit of God are children of God. For you did not receive a spirit of slavery to fall back into fear, but you have received a spirit of adoption. When we cry, 'Abba! Father!' it is that very Spirit bearing witness with our spirit that we are children of God, and if children, then heirs, heirs of God and joint heirs with Christ – if, in fact, we suffer with him so that we may also be glorified with him.*

Romans 8:14–17

Jesus did not leave his followers with the loneliness of their memories. He promised, before his death, to send a comforter, an advocate, a memory giver. One who, Jesus said, 'will remind you of all that I have said to you' (John 14:26). The Spirit was – and is – essential to the followers of Christ, marking a new age in which God pours out his Spirit on all who ask him, giving people an opportunity to know him in a deep and profound way.

At the Jewish festival of Pentecost, the holy breath of God enflamed the followers of Jesus – to the astonishment of those around them. The Church was born. It was a Church entrusted with the memory of Jesus. It was to be the carrier of his gospel, a body of believers in whom the Holy Spirit dwelt, marked by an identity found in Jesus Christ. They were to harness the power of recall by living and sharing the good news they had received.

In this, as with everything they did, the Holy Spirit of God was to be their empowerer, their enabler, the means by which they remembered Jesus' words. Jesus gifted his Church with the divine presence of the remembering Spirit, who would always glorify the Father through the Son. Through the Spirit, we are reminded of who we are.

Who Are We?

In the writings of the New Testament, we read about a young, growing church, learning from the teaching of her leaders, from experience, from encounter and yes, from mistakes. The early church needed to be reminded constantly of the source of her identity, just as we do today, as the collective people of God.

This collective and individual identity is more than a ticked box. Our identities are *fuelled* by who we are in Christ. The Holy Spirit testifies to this. We have been clothed with Christ, and yet so often we forget what we are supposed to be wearing and add items of our own – unhelpful things, *earthly things*, things that are old and muddied, instead of making the most of our brand new wardrobe.

If we disengage with the reality of our life in Christ, life becomes dislocated and compartmentalised. Our behaviour is out of sync with who we are called to be. In the New Testament, we're taught to put off our old self and to 'be renewed in the spirit of your minds', to 'clothe yourselves with the new self, created according to the likeness of God in true righteousness and holiness' (Ephesians 4:23–24). We're to live out this identity with every inch of our being, in all our comings and goings.

Mixed-up Memories

> So if you have been raised with Christ, seek the things that are above, where Christ is, seated at the right hand of God. Set your minds on things that are above, not on things that are on earth, for you have died, and your life is hidden with Christ in God. When Christ who is your life is revealed, then you also will be revealed with him in glory.
>
> Colossians 3:1–4

The early church communities had their problems, just as ours do. When the Galatians got their theology messed up and started clinging to human stipulations and the badges of the old covenant, Paul was incensed: 'I am astonished that you are so quickly deserting the one who called you to live in the grace of Christ and are turning to a different gospel – which is really no gospel at all' (Galatians 1:6, NIV). He goes on later: 'You foolish Galatians! Who has bewitched you? Before your very eyes Jesus Christ was clearly portrayed as crucified' (3:1, NIV). They were placing their identity back in old covenant rules instead of the new promise, insisting on observing aspects of the law (circumcision, for example). But what God had done in Christ had changed everything. It was this they were to rely on – nothing more, nothing less. It was by believing in this gospel that they had received the life-giving Spirit, not by doing the works of the law.[24]

The law was 'only a shadow of the good things to come and not the true form of these realities' (Hebrews 10:1). Because of Christ's

[24] Galatians 3:2–5.

once-for-all sacrifice, these shadows were shown to be what they were – they were not the real thing, they simply pointed towards it. The Galatians were walking back towards the signpost, instead of enjoying the reality of their destination – freedom in Christ: 'There is no longer Jew or Greek, there is no longer slave or free, there is no longer male and female; for all of you are one in Christ Jesus' (Galatians 3:28).

Those trying to persuade the new church that it needed to keep in line with the old ways may have believed their way was right, but when faced with their arguments, the joyful Christians in Galatia and other places were in danger of forgetting what they had previously accepted and celebrated. These garbled versions of the gospel muddied and dimmed their memories. Instead of forgetting that which was behind them, and pressing on to what was ahead,[25] they were dwelling on the former things, prior to the incarnation of Christ and the outpouring of the Holy Spirit – old memories which needed to be infused with the new. They needed to regain their perspective and not be side-tracked. They were in danger of forgetting the very thing that made them *who they now were*.

What happens when we can't remember, when gaps open in our memories? Often without realising, we try and fill the gaps with guesses of what should be there. The 'maybes' get bigger and the certainties recede. Before we know it, rusty memory has become faulty memory, and we're passing on our 'guesses in the gaps' to others. Eventually the whole thing seems unconvincing. Can we really be surprised?

We start to doubt what we have heard. Consider the story of the serpent in the garden of Eden: 'Did God say…?' He asks Eve.[26] Often we wonder: *Did God really say…? Have I got it right?*

When we start guessing in the gaps, we often say things that reflect more of ourselves, our traditions or our culture than they do of God and his ways. We supplement the holes in our memories with other, alien things. Without constant memory checks, these mistakes go unnoticed, until one day they are rampant. We need vibrant reminders of the Big Story, reminders that keep our memories fresh and full of grace.

[25] Philippians 3:13.
[26] Genesis 3:1.

Memory as Teacher

> Now I should remind you, brothers and sisters, of the good news
> that I proclaimed to you, which you in turn received, in which
> also you stand, through which also you are being saved, if you
> hold firmly to the message that I proclaimed to you – unless you
> have come to believe in vain.

1 Corinthians 15:1–2

We don't practise the heavily oral tradition of some societies, but we
still pass on information. In this small way, we are all teachers. This
is especially true of those growing up in the Christian faith. Family
and friends become our teachers, and we in turn become teachers
to others. Whenever we pass on an element of our faith, we are in
one sense teaching someone else. But things can get muddled, like
a series of Chinese whispers. This is even more the case now that
we live in an age of mass communication, where there are so many
different vehicles for our voices to find expression.

We're called to pass on our message. Is what we're saying
good and true? Have we grasped the true gospel or are we making
the same mistakes as the Galatians did – abandoning it for a diluted
or a legalistic version? We need constantly to review what we're
learning and what we're teaching. Remember James' warning
about the power of the tongue.[27] What memories are we making in
the minds of others? Do we make them feel they have to tick every
box in order to be acceptable to God or, conversely, tell them that
behaviour doesn't matter at all?

Paul's letters and the other New Testament writings often
addressed circumstances as they arose in the early church. They
were also in the business of reminding these new believers of who
they were to follow and to keep in step with the Spirit. Reminding
them of how they were to live. Reminding them that the two
were related and that who they were in Christ should inform their
lifestyles.

Together We Pray...

> Cast all your anxiety on him, because he cares for you.

1 Peter 5:7

[27] James 3.

These growing Christians were called to develop a pattern of living that centred around Jesus Christ, through loving each other, serving, helping those in need, and through prayer. Prayer was a staple of their lives. Anything – big or small – was to be taken to the God who cared for them and listened to them. They were to pray constantly, in the Spirit, with 'all kinds of prayers and requests'.[28]

They were also to encourage each other and not give up meeting together. They found strength from one another. More than this, being together helped keep their memories intact. They prayed together and for each other. In praying they were never alone, for the Spirit was with them to intercede with 'sighs too deep for words'.[29]

The power of recall was found in so many things – the teachings (and later writings) of witnesses to Christ, the prayers and fellowship of the believers, study of the Scriptures and, most importantly, through the presence of the Holy Spirit among them – the seal of their salvation and of their lives' purpose.

Remembering our God-given identity is essential. As we recall and reflect on what has been done for us, what memories are we making and how do they affect our lives? If we fail to recall who we are, what has been done for us and the reality of God in the life of the world, we get twisted by worry and doubt, throttled by all the things pulling at us, and confused by things that *sound* as if they should be true, even if they're not. The reasons behind what we say and do get blurry. We get in the habit of forgetting, and it shows.

Have I, unintentionally
been playing in the shadows
instead of dancing
in the light?
Lingering by the signpost,
rather than running towards
the destination?
Carer, Saviour, Friend –
call me onward.
Help me know your Spirit.
Help me seek your face.

[28] Ephesians 6:18, NIV.
[29] Romans 8:26.

FOR REFLECTION

- How might our churches be encountering issues similar or equivalent to those of the early church?
- What is 'the gospel'? Try describing it and then reflect on this description. Are there any gaps? How should this good news be expressed, in word and in action?
- How have you seen the Spirit's guiding – in your own life, the lives of others or the life of the Church?

Part III

Ripples of Forgetfulness

Chapter 11
Life Signs

Abide in me as I abide in you. Just as the branch cannot
bear fruit by itself unless it abides in the vine, neither
can you unless you abide in me. I am the vine, you are
the branches. Those who abide in me and I in them bear
much fruit, because apart from me you can do nothing.
John 15:4–5

Remembering God is not about one-day-a-week worship. Attending services or observing festivals and milestones may help us, but these are the signposts, not the destination. Paul was angry that the Galatians went back to observing special days, as if doing this earned God's favour. Even under the Old Covenant law, these were not the most important things. The prophet Amos recorded Yahweh as saying he *hated* the people's religious feasts and offerings, because they lived in a way that dishonoured these things.[30] Without care of the weak and poor, without justice, our remembering is flawed and vacant. We do not truly 'remember' in that active, mindful way when we behave in a way that does not reflect the character of God.

Showing God to the World
Corruption, injustice and apathy do not perform 'God music'. They are selfish little ditties of our own, not accurate reflections of the great symphony of God's love, mercy and justice. They are expressions of forgetful hearts – both individual and collective. Forgetful hearts cushion themselves with their own concerns. Whether caught by quiet apathy or inner turmoil, their radar is not picking up that which is beyond themselves. Such forgetfulness ripples outwards. Knowledge of our faith needs to shape and form us – if we distance it from our lifestyles, we are still forgetting:

[30] See Amos 5:21–24.

Forgetting that our God is a God of justice and of mercy.

Forgetting that our God is a God of love and of compassion.

Forgetting that our God is angered and grieved by the pain and abuse in this world.

Forgetting that our God sees us – all of us – and knows all our deeds, and also the lack of them.

Forgetting that our calling is not merely individual but collective, meant to impact the world around us, meant to *change* things.

If we forget God, what hope is there for our world? Memory is part of our witness, our purpose. When we ignore the needs of others, we forget the character of our God. We sign our names on the dotted line, but neglect to re-read the document. Is the 'job description' accurately reflected in our lives? When we see inconsistencies do we try to change the job description or suggest a different way of reading it, instead of facing up to its challenges? Do we dare tone down *God*?

Faith Shown in Action

For it is by grace you have been saved, through faith – and this is not from yourselves, it is the gift of God – not by works, so that no one can boast. For we are God's handiwork, created in Christ Jesus to do good works, which God prepared in advance for us to do.

Ephesians 2:8–10 (NIV)

Suppose a brother or sister is without clothes and daily food. If one of you says to him, 'Go in peace; keep warm and well fed,' but does nothing about their physical needs, what good is it?

James 2:15–16

We are saved by grace through faith, but faith without deeds is dead. We cannot work our own way into God's kingdom; God's grace alone does that – through the life, death and resurrection of the Son. Faith in Christ is what identifies us as the people of God. Despite this, if we profess a faith that does nothing and affects nothing, it is not living faith. *We are created in Christ to do good works.* Our Christ-identity is designed to be reflected in the way we live. It's a question that has whispered to me for years: *what if we really lived what we said we believed?* Do we pay no attention to all that Jesus taught and embodied during his time among us? Do we pick and mix his teaching, choosing only the comfortable bits? We are known by our fruits, so what happens when we are fruitless?

Some reading this may immediately go into a journey of self-condemnation. Panic ensues – *help! I'm fruitless!* Is my faith dead? This panic is usually a sign that it is not! Yes, we all struggle. Yes, we may *feel* fruitless but God can use us in ways we cannot imagine. Every attempt we make for God's kingdom, however muddled and fearful, is a sign of a living faith. We do not always perceive the outcome of these attempts but God sees them and values our acts of remembering.

The tragedy is not when we stop 'succeeding' in our own eyes but when we stop trying. Overwhelmed, our vision becomes clouded by a sense of our own uselessness. This in itself is another form of forgetting: forgetting the value that God has given us, forgetting that we are defined by him, not our own circumstances. Whether through a careless or 'dead' faith, or a faith mourning its apparent lack of productivity, we stall. The causes and the triggers of these are very different and will require different solutions.

The Big Freeze

So, thinking about 'dead' faith – the faith without works that James talks about, what can we say? Here are a few suggestions of how this might look (remembering of course that only God sees the heart).

- What we profess to believe has no impact on our lives.
- Our characters do not mirror any 'God' qualities – and we're not troubled by the fact.
- Compassion and kindness are markedly absent.
- God is confined to the box ticked 'religion' and does not affect any other 'categories' in life – be it work, relationships or leisure.
- We are paralysed by apathy.

What about what I'm calling a 'frozen' faith?

- Attempts at helping and changing the lives of others have been met with misunderstanding or hostility, and we've grown disillusioned.

- Crises of confidence mean we freeze, uncertain of how to act.
- We grieve over what we cannot do.
- We perceive the negative aspects of our characters and long to change but have given up on our ability to do so.
- We are paralysed by pain and anxiety.

A 'dead' faith will usually deny that it is dead. A faith frozen by circumstance will constantly worry that it is dead. Both forget the source of change and strength, but a dead faith doesn't really want to 'plug in'. A frozen faith tries to do it all, forgets to plug in and then sinks into despair.

Whose Fruit Is It Anyway?

In the Gospel of John, Jesus describes himself as the vine, sustaining the connecting branches. If a branch is detached from the parent plant, there is no source of life for it, and it will shrivel and die. In this vivid analogy, it is clear that remaining connected to *Jesus* is the key to our lives bearing fruit. Our efforts draw from the strength of the vine and we bear *his* fruit in our lives.[31]

As we've seen in earlier chapters, we often measure our lives by our achievements. That may be what we would call the fruit of our lives, but is this Kingdom fruit? What did Jesus mean when he talked of bearing 'good' fruit instead of 'bad'?[32] What *are* the good deeds that show faith is alive and vibrant?

Often we can get sucked into a tick box culture. Our lives begin to feel like forms we need to fill in. Either we get so caught up in the things we have 'ticked' that we end up swamped by ambition and pride, or we get consumed by the empty boxes – the missing 'ticks' – and disillusionment and disappointment become our masters. Isn't it true that the fruits – the achievements – in the eyes of the world around us are rarely the same as Kingdom values? Consider the fruit of the memory-giving Spirit – one multi-flavoured fruit comprising of love, joy, peace, patience, kindness, goodness (or generosity), faithfulness, gentleness and self-control.[33] How often do we think of ticking off these?

We can become so task-driven, doing what 'needs to be done', that we forget to focus on the attitude behind our lives. We slot

[31] See John 15.
[32] Matthew 7:17.
[33] Galatians 5:22–23.

'faith' and 'deeds' into separate categories when they are meant to be one organic whole. We are not meant to be driven by the need to achieve or to prove ourselves to the world. Instead the love of Christ compels us.[34] Whose fruit is it anyway? Is the way we live a reflection of God's way – of the values of the Kingdom, of the fruit of the Spirit? Or are we working to a different template – one that puffs us up or tears us down?

Perhaps we need a new checklist, one not based solely on the tasks ahead but focusing on the way we approach our lives. Not all of us are in the position to be as active as we'd like, but we can still reflect the character of Christ, even within our limitations. Are we kind, loving and gentle? Are we driven by our own desires and opinions or by the beautiful, compelling love of Christ?

Transforming Grace

Dead faith does not care; frozen faith is consumed by care. In the first instance, we need to be challenged to understand that our faith is not truly living faith unless it impacts our lives, that following Jesus has never been about lip service but about the practical outworking of what we believe and what it means to be connected to him.

In the second instance, we need to be challenged to understand that we do not rely on our own strength. All that we do for God is in response to his grace and his mercies, which are new every morning.[35] We have let ourselves become trapped by the memory makers of worry and fear. We need to examine our loyalties and reaffirm *who* we follow and all that he has promised. We need to stop looking inward and constantly analysing ourselves, and look up – and then out.

In all cases, we need to remind ourselves that it is God's grace that transforms us.

*Lord sometimes I wish I was
so many different things.
So capable of This and That,
those tasks that others
seem to excel at.*

[34] 2 Corinthians 5:14.
[35] Lamentations 3:23.

Sometimes I fear my life
will never match their template;
I feel impaired by all the things
I cannot do or ever do.

But you call me to a different
rhythm, a pattern made
of different colours.
It's your fruit I want to show,
not theirs.

Your love. Your joy.
Your taste, vibrant and energising
in a weary world.

FOR REFLECTION

- Is your faith careless or consumed by care? Or neither? What makes you think this?
- How might you need to readdress your understanding of grace? Try writing your own definition.
- List the flavours of the fruit of the Spirit from Galatians 5:22–23. Note which ones you find particularly difficult.
- Which of these flavours have you seen exemplified by others? How was this shown?

He has told you, O mortal, what is good;
and what does the LORD require of you
but to do justice, and to love kindness,
and to walk humbly with your God?
Micah 6:8

Chapter 12
Compassion Fatigue

Arise, cry out in the night, as the watches of the night begin;
pour out your heart like water in the presence of the Lord.
Lift up your hands to him for the lives of your children,
who faint from hunger at every street corner.
Lamentations 2:19 (NIV)

Sometimes we forget because it's necessary. We need to survive, to cope with daily life, to move on from the things that limit or hurt us. All memory is selective; this is not always a bad thing. The question is, are we selecting the *right* things to remember? For example, we've already considered how our worries focus on unhelpful things.

Shutting Down

There are things in our lives it is good to forget. God is a master of deliberate forgetting – wiping our sins from the slate of his memory so that they no longer stand between us. Deliberate forgetting is sometimes necessary and entirely understandable. Even so, sometimes it becomes merely an act of defence, a reaction against overload. Along with all the trivial bits of information that assail us, we also shut out the suffering of the world. We close our minds to the cries of the victims of violence, abuse and oppression. We forget, because we feel we have to.

Our minds naturally filter out some information, subconsciously weighing importance and unimportance. If this did not happen we would feel constantly bombarded by everything we experience and remember experiencing in the past. An inability to forget makes a normal life impossible to live. However, sometimes we deliberately turn our eyes away from things, not because they are trivial but because they trouble us too deeply. We learn to deflect them, because we do not know how to carry them with us all the time.

This, of course, is what God does. God carries and hears the pain of the world in a way we cannot comprehend, with a knowledge so vast in comparison to ours that there are no words big enough to try and encapsulate it. We are not God, and our hands are so small. How then, do we remember without being overwhelmed?

In a world of mass communication and globalisation, we are no longer concerned only with the events that occur in our own locality or region, or even in our own country. We have a whole world's worth of news constantly tugging at our attention, and a whole world's worth of suffering to comprehend. A sudden disaster and its repercussions, a long-running war with no end in sight or the hopelessness of a crumbling society facing continual violence and lawlessness – any and all of these add up to form a sobering and overwhelming cascade of human suffering.

A kind of paralysis takes place. We can't comprehend what we are seeing and hearing about. We become numb to the images we see every day. We no longer react to stories of extreme suffering or natural disasters. Poverty, inequality, violence, abuse … we shut it off, unable to deal with it or even feel the need to address it. We fall prey to compassion fatigue.

Finding a Voice

When God spoke to me about my own compassion fatigue, it was through a series of events, images and words which were brought to my attention over time. All were needed to soften a much-hardened heart. It was not hardened by callousness or cruelty, but because I felt unable to make a difference, especially owing to my fluctuating energy levels. All the suffering of the world felt distant to me because of its enormity. Eventually, however, a melting took place, and I felt the breaking of God's heart in my own.

I realised that in not feeling able to do everything or even much at all, we end up doing nothing. We forget about the small things we can do because they do not seem enough. One by one we step back, out of the arena, until there are only a few left to bear the burden of caring for our world.

As a baby born in the late nineteenth century, Helen Keller was struck by an illness that left her both deaf and blind. She lived in a world of darkness until a woman called Annie Sullivan, herself only partially sighted, taught her to communicate by using her fingers to 'spell' on another's palms. Despite being denied two out of five senses, with great perseverance, Helen eventually learned how to speak. In her lecture tours, which took her round the world, she promoted the welfare and better treatment of the deaf and blind, as well as writing several books about her own life. She who was both blind and deaf found a voice, enabling others to see.

We differ, blind and seeing, one from another: not in our senses, but in the use we make of them. Here am I, both seeing and hearing, but so often I close my eyes and block my ears and refuse to use my perfectly capable voice. We don't know what to pray, so we end up not praying. We don't know what to give, so we give nothing. We don't know what to do, so we don't do anything.

In an unjust world, we may ache when we see and hear of suffering. All the same, we tend to lose steam, our hearts crowded by forgetfulness and weariness. We get distracted, forgetting the importance of our cause, forgetting the ache of compassion, becoming jaded at what feel like such futile attempts to change the world.

My own attempts involved something I loved doing – writing – at a time when poor health prevented me from participating in many areas of life. I collected various, relevant poems I had written, wrote some more, and compiled a simple anthology. In itself it carried the message of how important our actions are – however small – in a hurting world. By doing this, I managed to raise over £500 for the people of Darfur.

And I almost didn't do it.

Life with all its demands (valid or otherwise) continued to yell at me, and it was easy to become distracted. But this was something the Holy Spirit whispered into my heart, and it would not be dislodged. I had to keep praying that I would keep caring enough to do it.

We carry so many good intentions. We think that we will do something, say something, simply pray something – but so often we forget. It's in a world riddled by forgetfulness that we are called to remember. We are called to care.

Choosing to Care

We may think we cannot help a needy world because of our personal situations – the state of our health or finances, or other constricting circumstances. But at the very least we can act as rememberers, those who never give up pleading the cause of the orphan and the widow. Yes, the world is full of vast and desperate need. Yes, much of it will be beyond our individual help. But at the end of everything when the Son of God himself turns and asks, 'Why? Why did you do nothing?', will it really be good enough to say in response: 'I just didn't know where to start'?

Start anywhere. You want to say you did nothing because there was in essence *too much choice*? I'm writing to myself as much as anyone. I'm often overwhelmed, tempted to turn off, frequently unfeeling and unmoved, and underestimating what I can do in my own tiny sphere. These words are not thrown out as accusations but act as a self-summoning. I want to change. My heart is so hard.

Standing Together

We think so much in terms of the individual that we forget the collective power of doing – of contributing to something together. We are so tempted to separate into self-pitying bubbles of 'I can't do anything about this' that we forget we are part of a body. Those who do see it are frequently exhausted from trying to summon any kind of effort from those who are bubble-clad, having no desire to remember a world beyond their own private and personal journeys, their own private and personal fulfilment, their own private and personal relationship with God.

And yet the God with whom we have this relationship is not a cosy or a comfortable God. God hears the cries of the abused and the oppressed. Yes, he is the God who comforts us, but he also challenges us. We look around and try and find 'what is good for me' or 'where can I get this' or 'what meets my need' – a consumerist culture driving the desire to 'shop' for church and spirituality.

A child just died needlessly while you read that paragraph.

Give you a sickening jolt? Me too.

Start somewhere. Pray. Research an issue or a need and talk about it. You don't have to fix the whole world, just start remembering *something*. Talk until people have to listen and they start talking too. Together talk so loudly that those in power cannot help but hear you, and the cogs of action begin to turn. Yes, we are only human. No, we cannot do everything. But surely – *surely* – that doesn't mean we should do nothing at all. However little we possess, we can still give wholeheartedly.

It's not all about ability, either. Within those struggling with desperate limitations of poor health or difficult circumstances, there can still be the heart of a cheerful giver. For now, let's forget about the things we can't manage and think about the things we can.

We can give our time. We can give our prayers. We can give our minds, committing them to a more compassionate way of thinking. Our voices may feel small, shy and squeaky, but we can still use them to encourage others, to inspire others, to speak out on behalf of others. We can be advocates for those who have no voice at all.

Making Noise

'But woe to you Pharisees! For you tithe mint and rue and herbs of all kinds, and neglect justice and the love of God; it is these you ought to have practised, without neglecting the others.'

Luke 11:42

Despite the fact that we live in a world jam-packed with communication technologies, we can end up being more insular, not less. We cling to the digital realities in which we immerse ourselves and the devices we cradle in our palms. We can forget to look beyond them. Our minds only cope with the bite-sized in life – complex situations merely puzzle us, the effort to understand being rejected as simply too much bother.

Our entertainment systems consume our time and thoughts – what we did at the weekend, what we watched, who we talked to on Facebook or Twitter. Ironically the more 'realistic' our stories, songs, soundbites and films become, the easier it can be to consign the suffering of others to a kind of fiction. It's something we are moved by, even cry at, but at the end of the viewing we can still finish our popcorn and go home, change channel or switch to another information feed.

Distracted by all the wonderful ways we can communicate, we can so easily become enamoured by the trivial, caught up in fiery debates about minor things, concerned with being the most witty, the most supposedly 'profound', the most re-tweetable. We are tempted to stand at our equivalent of the street corner, showing off how thoughtful, how kind, how very holy we are, not realising how we come across. The world is watching – one false move or unwise comment and a reputation is torn to shreds. We often use our voices only to criticise or mock, not harnessing the power for good that our technology offers us, but squandering it in a constant crossfire of approval and disapproval. If, instead, we choose to use these things in a way that makes a genuinely worthwhile noise, we can make a difference.

In a world so full of communication the potential for noise-making is immense. Let's go viral with justice-talk, with compassion, not with barbed retorts and constant condemnation. Let's not shut up about the things that matter. The Old Testament prophets didn't. John the Baptist didn't. Jesus didn't, and neither did his first disciples. We are *called* to be makers of peace, bringers of justice, carriers of compassion. At no point can we fling in the towel when there is still injustice in our world.

When reading the Old Testament prophets, it's clear that injustice and oppression is characteristic of forgetting and abandoning Yahweh. The prophets are outraged at those who crush the poor and needy while boasting of the lip service they pay to Yahweh. In the New Testament, Jesus was infuriated that those in religious leadership were so neglectful of their roles, not merely as law-keepers but as justice bearers.

Can we really consign this to *then* and not apply it to *now*? Belief in Yahweh was not merely about saying he existed; that was accepted. Neither was it merely about displays of worship, prayers or offerings. It was about displaying his character, acting according to his ways, propagating truth, mercy and justice. It was about *living* the faith, not merely ascribing to it. It was about active, compassionate remembering.

Canvas

inspire me.
do not leave me
in my world
of waste,
the place
where I crawl
inside my own
apathy.

strengthen me.
do not let me give in
to the voices
which say

forget
what you do –
you will never change
the world.

remind me.
that on a painting
composed
entirely of black
one tiny streak
of brilliant white
can change the whole
picture.[36]

FOR REFLECTION

- What things have we chosen to ignore because they're just too hard to face?
- Make a list of the things that concern you. Pray about them, and brainstorm ideas of how you could help – however small these may be.
- What would you like to be remembered for? What do you wish your obituary will say?

---

[36] This is a poem I used for my anthology, my little attempt at making a difference, which also encapsulated the feeling behind it.

'I give you a new commandment, that you love one another. Just as I have loved you, you also should love one another. By this everyone will know that you are my disciples, if you have love for one another.'
John 13:34–35

Chapter 13

Remembering and Relationships

... be kind to one another, tender-hearted,
forgiving one another,
as God in Christ has forgiven you.
Ephesians 4:32

'That's just the way I am,' she said. 'People have to accept that.'

I was sitting with someone who'd had an argument with a friend, listening as she explained the reason for the disagreement. I didn't reply to her comments, but I was unconvinced then, and I'm unconvinced now. The idea that we can't change clashes with my worldview. Yet we frequently come to our relationships with this feeling, even if it is only subconscious. We carry a kind of 'take me or leave me' attitude, resenting those who think we should be different.

Perceptions of Reality

Sometimes people's expectations of us *are* unreasonable. I often reflect that no human being is strong enough to take the weight of another for any real amount of time, and expecting someone to meet all our needs and get everything right is neither realistic nor fair. Only God has that kind of strength – and that kind of love. This doesn't mean that our faith shouldn't have a transforming effect on our lives – beyond the surface clutter to the deep-down 'self', the core of our characters. If remembering God means remembering others and treating them in a way that reflects God's character, our relationships should be deeply impacted by this kind of remembering.

It's so tempting to forget to behave lovingly to the ones we love the most. They get the worst of us. In a sense, this is inevitable. We will be open with one another in a way we are not with others, and our ugly bits will be less well hidden. But should they not also get the best of us? If we're saving the dregs, the grumpy bits, the oh-I'm-so-fed-up-with-life bits for those we consider most important in our lives and neglecting to give them the encouraging and positive bits, they're not getting a very good deal!

Relationships do not exist in a void. Our lives are full of reference points around which we structure ourselves, which is part of the reason why memory loss is so distressing. When our capacity to remember slips from us, we worry about all that we will lose. Memories are precious; they are much more than souvenirs or mementoes. These are only reminders, mere catalysts for remembering.

We don't change reality by what we remember, but the practice of remembering affects our perceptions of that reality. Likewise our memory and its loss cannot change the character of God – he is not confined by our limitations – but it affects our *perceptions* of God. In doing so, it impacts our relationship with him and with others.

Transforming Flavours

In Galatians 5, Paul describes the fruit of the Spirit. The word for 'fruit' is singular – it's not as if love is a banana and patience an apple. We can't leave self-control to one side, as if it were a bunch of seeded grapes when we only like the seedless variety. When someone takes a bite of us they should get the whole medley of flavours: love, joy, peace, patience, kindness, goodness/generosity, faithfulness, gentleness and self-control (note the mention of faithfulness, biblically often the opposing virtue to forgetfulness). The flavours work together, complementing each other. When one is lacking, the fruit doesn't taste as good as it should. It's clear from the passage in Galatians that Paul is endorsing these things *instead* of the ugly bits he talks about in the previous verses. We should be actively seeking to produce these flavours in our lives.

If we don't seek to inhabit the new beliefs and the new behaviours, old beliefs and old behaviours can hang around unhelpfully. Paul talks of the conflict we experience between the 'sinful nature' and the fruit of the Spirit and instructs his readers to 'keep in step with the Spirit' (Galatians 5:25, NIV). We act out God's way for us. We can't be disciples on auto-pilot.

We can dismiss our behaviour, even our core characters, as being set in stone. This is untrue. Our brains are capable of forming whole new connections and patterns of behaviour. We *can* change the way we think and behave, even if the process is a tough one.[37] Put God and his transforming power into the mix and everything takes on a whole new light. We are full of potential for change, for transformation, for a whole new set of flavours.

Sometimes the belief that we can't change can seem so fixed that we don't even try to look beyond it. We need to confront that belief and give it a good talking to. We are not lost causes; we are never without hope. This is something we need to bear in mind as we explore our behaviours and the way we treat others.

Our True Condition

> By dint of will people can make a good showing for a time, but sooner or later there will come that unguarded moment where the 'careless word' will slip out to reveal the true condition of the heart.
> Richard Foster[38]

In places of safety, we show our true selves. We display our vulnerability and our hurt, and reveal our less desirable tendencies. Inevitably, these will spill out into the lives of others – most frequently affecting those we love the most. How does our remembering affect us at these points of vulnerability and disagreeability?

The way we treat each other reveals not just our attitudes to one another but our attitudes to God. 'Those who say, "I love God", and hate their brothers or sisters, are liars; for those who do not love a brother or sister whom they have seen, cannot love God whom they have not seen' (1 John 4:20). By treating those around us with love and respect, we demonstrate our love for God. In the language of this book, we remember God.

Jesus said that whatever we do for the 'least of these' – those who are hungry, poor and in need – we do for him. Our relationships with others are vital in our service to Christ. We often forget this. We don't actively recall how we should treat others, in moments when everything is going wrong, when we're tired, ill, irritable or unhappy. Remembering in these moments is a challenge to all of us. I admire those who manage to remain kind and loving even when the world is falling about them – they are true witnesses to

---

[37] This is explored further in chapter 19.

[38] Richard Foster, Celebration of Discipline (Hodder and Stoughton, 1989), revised edition, p. 6. Copyright © 1989 by Richard Foster; reproduced by permission of the publisher Hodder and Stoughton.

the God who made them in his image. I'm painfully aware of how easy it is for me to forget to love my neighbour.

Grace under Pressure

It's even harder when those around us don't treat us lovingly. When metaphorically pinned in a corner by a tirade of criticism or ill-tempered words, it's embarrassing how easy it is to be ill-tempered or even cruel ourselves. Even if we manage not to say them out loud, our thoughts about that person can become less and less kind. We can forget in these moments that God alone sets our value, that this person, for all their negativity and fury, cannot undo our worth. Jesus didn't just tell us to love our neighbours; he told us to love our *enemies*. In a sense, we are called to go against our instincts – instincts fuelled by anger and hurt – and create new instincts, new responses, new patterns of behaviour.

This includes every sphere of our lives. It applies to our interactions with spouses, parents, children and siblings. It applies to those we follow and interact with on social media, to the friends we've known for most of our lives and the ones we've only just met. It includes the stranger on the doorstep, calling at an inconvenient time; it includes those who irritate us, ignore us or bait us.

Trying to focus on God and what he wants of us in moments of hurtful negativity takes a great deal of strength and practice. We will often get it wrong before we start getting it right. The practice of remembering God in our lives can help us in these moments if we do, indeed, practise. Just as we require discipline to sit at a piano, stumbling over wrong notes or playing in the wrong time, we need to keep working at our reactions to others. We will get it wrong. However, the more we attempt to play our music for God in our relationships with others, the more embedded the melody will become.

Watch Your Reflexes

Changing our reflex reactions can be a challenge. Remember Nehemiah and his reaction to those mocking his wall?[39] Nehemiah responds with a prayer: 'Hear us, O our God, for we are despised' (Nehemiah 4:4).When we are despised it's very easy to lash out at those doing the despising, to match scorn with scorn. But Nehemiah prays. It's not a perfect prayer, or a politically correct prayer, but it takes his hurt and his anger to God, who can handle it. What is

[39] See chapter 8 of this book.

your reflex reaction when someone criticises or hurts you? Do you respond in kind – whether in full-blown rage, sarcasm or malice? Or do you remember who God has called you to be?

This does not mean we condone or allow abusive behaviour. Nehemiah took measures to defend the wall because he perceived genuine danger. But if he had responded in kind – by throwing back insults and making his own violent threats, he might well have exacerbated the situation. A wounded animal will lash out when a hurting place is knocked and so, too, can we. Those we love are those most able to cause us pain. They know where it hurts. When those we trust are those who hit us in that place, the shockwaves follow. Conflict in close relationships is incredibly painful. When we get into a word-war or a long-term argument, the damage can be great. It distracts us from our purpose. In effect, like the people of Jerusalem in the days of Nehemiah, we stop building the wall.

Perhaps we don't retaliate in this way. Perhaps we let the words sink into us and allow them to form us. Perhaps we begin to believe them, and forget what we used to know. Mired in doubt and depression, we huddle ourselves around our hurt and hope that we can hold it together. Our efforts are undermined. Our sense of purpose diminishes. We forget what we're here for; we forget what we're called to do.

Are there things in our lives we have forgotten about? Dreams, aspirations, things we wanted so much to do for God – and felt he wanted us to do – but somehow they've got lost in all the rubbish? All we encountered was indifference and opposition, and we lost heart. We stopped building the wall.

It's naïve to think that words do not hurt, or that we are unaffected by them. If I'm angry, it's often because I'm hurt. Knowing the reasons for our reactions allows us to watch ourselves more closely. We need to watch our reflexes, especially when it hurts the most. Our reflex reactions can be just as damaging, and make bridges, as well as walls, harder to repair.

Perhaps we do what Nehemiah did – pray reflexively, reactively – throwing the hurt into a safe place, avoiding further repercussions. Trusting in one who is bigger than our pain and our confusion. Being honest about how we feel, ugly as it may be. It's okay to be honest with God. God knows – and loves us – anyway.

We need to ask ourselves: am I chained by my personal history, allowing past hurts to dictate future actions? What and who defines me? How is this affecting my relationships?

That Same Old Record Again!

I know I've repeated this throughout and you're probably tired of hearing it. The remembering that God calls us to do is an act of *consciously recalling*. The memory loss I'm describing is not really nuts-and-bolts remembering – although this can help us in our thinking – but a heart cry, a faith need, something that runs deep within us.

This kind of remembering will – and should – impact those close to us. They should be our frontline witnesses, seeing the efforts we make to treat them with love and respect, even when we're struggling. These efforts to remember within our closest relationships impact the quality of those relationships. We're to reflect God in our relationships, mirroring the grace, love and forgiveness we've received in the way we interact with those around us.

Walk with Me

*Walk with me
when friendship feels
tangible, faith
touchable and able
to wrap us in a blanket
when the wind is
brisk, and carries
flecks of winter*

*Walk with me
when love's adhesive
does not stick and hope
is landlocked, what then?
Then walk with me
though fingers graze
sharp-edged stones –
one thing is known.*

Together is better than alone.

FOR REFLECTION

- What are your most common reflex reactions? What triggers them?
- What relationships are you struggling with at the moment?
- What do you need to work on in these specific situations?

Finally, beloved, whatever is true, whatever is honourable,
whatever is just, whatever is pure, whatever is pleasing,
whatever is commendable, if there is any excellence
and if there is anything worthy of praise,
think about these things.
Philippians 4:8

Chapter 14
Memory and Mastery

For if any are hearers of the word and not doers, they are like those who look at themselves in a mirror; for they look at themselves and, on going away, immediately forget what they were like.

James 1:23–24

Faithful Memory

In many ways, memory is directional, linking us to different experiences, places and times. It looks beyond itself to something else. Faith, too, is directional, not an object or even a subject, but active. It is faith that *does* the believing, the trusting, the hoping in something beyond itself.

If our memories and faith don't impact our lives, we end up like those described in James 1, looking in a mirror, but immediately forgetting what we've seen. In the biblical stories, faithfulness is often the opposite of forgetfulness. Faithlessness *is* forgetfulness, and vice versa. The two interweave and overlap. So – if faithlessness is equated with forgetfulness, can we do the opposite and equate faith with memory? It could be said that faith itself is an act of memory. It's a kind of remembering that looks forward as well as back, actualising past events in the present and allowing them to inform the future, based on previous experience or received promises.

The direction of our faith-remembering impacts the way we live, revealing the true state of our hearts and minds. What comes out of us is symptomatic of what is within. 'Above all else, guard your heart, for everything you do flows from it,' says a writer of Proverbs (4:23, NIV).

Only One Rescuer

See, the LORD's hand is not too short to save, nor his ear too dull to hear.

Isaiah 59:1

Negative memories can bring us great pain, causing us to relive moments of past hurt, brokenness, abuse and loss. Is there a way to stop these memories controlling us, especially in the dark, unfettered places where we lose our grip? Can we allow the greater remembering of our faith to heal and to soften, to weave in hope and light amid the darkness, to turn our thoughts in a different direction?

These are questions not easily answered, because every situation is different and deeply personal. We can plunge clumsily into a situation full of grief and damage and our presumptions of healing can lead some to despair. So it is with caution we address such things: the bad memories, the shocking memories, memories that warp and destroy. There is no room for judgement here, only compassion. We must handle the issue of traumatic memory with care, recognising the sheer 'badness' of a situation while acknowledging the full goodness of God.

Sometimes we long to snap our fingers or wave a wand and make things better, but God often works slowly – more slowly than *we* think he should, perhaps, offering opportunities for healing but not forcing them, where we would want to *make* things right – there and then. Our hurry to help can make those in question feel guilty for *not* fitting the mould, giving in to pretending that everything is all right when it really isn't. This inevitably leads to problems later; trying to paint over the cracks only masks them temporarily. They are still there and, as the paint peels away, they can seem even uglier than before.

We do not always make the best rescuers. It is God who specialises in rescue, overcoming darkness, providing redemption from slavery and freedom for those imprisoned – whether their chains are seen or unseen. It is God who makes new memories, more powerful than the old. Through the power of the Holy Spirit, God transforms us from the inside out. This God is a saviour utterly unlike our old masters, be they actual people, specific traumatic events or the more 'abstract' consequences – fear, anger, hate, bitterness, pain.

There will always be 'things' trying to clutter up the space of our lives, to fill the void – even if they are things that smack of nothingness. Apathy itself can become our master. But are our substitutes strong enough? Can they mend us, redeem is, remake us? Can they take on board all our hurts and our brokenness, and not be daunted by our messiness and our darkness? Are they equipped to understand and see us as we really are? And how much power do they have to change us into something better, to make a positive impact on the world around us?

> O Joy that seekest me through pain,
> I cannot close my heart to Thee;
> I trace the rainbow through the rain,
> And feel the promise is not vain,
> That morn shall tearless be.

> O Cross that liftest up my head,
> I dare not ask to fly from Thee;
> I lay in dust life's glory dead,
> And from the ground there blossoms red
> Life that shall endless be.

from *O Love that wilt not let me go*, George Matheson (1842–1906)

The Necessity of Forgetting

Just like remembering, forgetting is necessary in order to live productive lives. We need to filter out some things in order to operate. We *have* to forget some things, just as we have to remember others, otherwise we would live in continual overload. But do we filter out what we should have kept and keep what we should have filtered out? Are our thoughts tied up with worry, stress and ambition?

Why are some memories more vivid than others? It could be the significance of the event. It could be the emotional impact of an experience. Maybe it is heightened by a sense of nostalgia; we replay the memories with affection (or regret). Do we channel this nostalgia in a good way – using it to reassure and sustain us? Or does it disable us in the present, so that we are tempted to 'forget' what we have now?

Memory can be a source of both joy and pain. Sometimes the two are not separate but entwined. A beautiful memory can be tainted with sadness at the absence of a loved one. We would not wish to set aside the memory simply because it provokes sadness as well as joy. We may need to work through it, allowing ourselves to recognise that it was real, but so is this – here and now. We often edit memories, seeing only the negatives, forgetting the moments of blessing or, conversely, forgetting the difficulties and focusing only on the joys.

Impossibly Golden?

We often remember things altogether more rosily than they were – consider the exiled Israelites longing for the golden days of Solomon. Yes, our memories are incredibly valuable in informing our identities, relationships and purpose, but do we use them to fuel us towards future hope? Or do we simply spend our time daydreaming of days gone by, giving them an impossibly golden hue? The reality is that life is many-hued – full of multi-coloured moments that mould us, inspire us, weary us or grieve us.

Sometimes I've read back over what I've written in past journals and realised it *wasn't* all that rosy. There were very difficult moments, and times when I wished I were somewhere (or some-when) else – even back then, in that supposed 'golden age'.

Milestones can be great encouragements. But we are not meant to hang them around our necks. We are encouraged to use our memories and our past experience to inform our present identity and to dream for the future.

Finding the Right Direction

What are our most powerful memories? What is it that weighs on us, whether conscious or not, in the morning, the afternoon and the evening? What plays at the edges of our night-time dreaming? Forgetfulness creates a void, but it does not stay empty. What are we allowing to replace our faithful remembering? What crowds in and influences our thoughts, actions and words? What, when we forget, are we choosing to remember instead?

When God is absent from our remembering, we dwell on other things, other people. Who are our masters, and our idols? Who receives the sacrifices of our hearts, the offerings of our lives? To whom – or what – do we give our time, our commitment, our love and our need? What do we think about in moments of busyness or moments of quietness? Again, so many questions, and again, the answers are not easy.

Memory in the Digital Age

We live in a gadget- and network-driven society. Many of these things can be useful to us, acting as triggers for remembering, helplines for the lonely and ways of connecting that 50 years ago would have seemed impossible.

But if we took away all this technology, what would we remember? How much more are we struggling to concentrate? Have we invested all our remembering into outside sources – are they only backups, or are we no longer the carriers of our own cultural and religious memories? Are we so glued to our gadgets that we don't know how to stick to anything else? There are plenty of opportunities for distraction in this digital age, and an increasing array of choices in how we live our lives.

Let's not forget where we're supposed to be fixing our gaze. We need to ensure we don't rely too much on other media for our remembering, and be aware of how they affect our concentration – an integral part of memory formation.

We can get addicted to our gadgets. We live in an age where this is increasingly common and a danger that should not be underestimated – am I bothering to learn and remember things, beyond that small and yet so compelling screen? We can think that, with such distracted minds, our gadgets are lifesavers – helping us remember where we struggled before. But within this assumption we need to understand that the less we do something, the harder it becomes. Are we lost without the things we have come to rely on as our memory keepers? If we 'outsource' all our memories, we may forget how to remember for ourselves. We need to work at retaining and embedding our most important memories, so that should all the reminders be taken away, we are not left with nothing.

Forgetfulness Is Easy

Is it possible, I wonder, to worship nothingness? Can emptiness itself be our master? When there are gaps in our lives and our remembering that remain unfilled, they loiter around our lifestyles and drum out a rhythm of their own. Forgetfulness has its own soundtrack. And it doesn't think to look out for the needs of others or live out godly love in a tired world.

Words like loss, lack and missing are all describing realities, however abstract they may be. They are all opposites – of having, of gaining, of experience, of *presence*. Forgetfulness itself becomes our master, and we feel unwilling to switch our allegiance. It becomes easier to forget, easier not to care, easier not to remember who we are called to be.

How can we worship God when we have forgotten God?

And there's always so much
to think about and sometimes
I can't recall
just how I got here
So many things
tugging
tugging
tugging
until I am no longer sure
of anything, I am
just a selection
of tiny
pieces

FOR REFLECTION

- What bad memories still affect you today? Where do you long for God's healing touch?
- Conversely, are you enamoured by the past? How can you embrace God's promises for the present and the future, without being trapped by nostalgia?
- Try and identify the 'masters' in your life. What swallows up your time? Where do you need to ration yourself?

*O give thanks to the L*ORD*, call on his name,*
make known his deeds among the peoples.
Sing to him, sing praises to him;
tell of all his wonderful works.
Glory in his holy name;
*let the hearts of those who seek the L*ORD *rejoice.*
*Seek the L*ORD *and his strength;*
seek his presence continually.
Remember the wonderful works he has done,
his miracles, and the judgements he has uttered…
Psalm 105:1–5

Chapter 15
Worship and Witness

Let us hold fast to the confession of our hope without wavering, for he who has promised is faithful. And let us consider how to provoke one another to love and good deeds, not neglecting to meet together, as is the habit of some, but encouraging one another, and all the more as you see the Day approaching.
Hebrews 10:23–25

Memory inspires worship. We worship God because we love God, and because we remember what God has done for us – both at the macro level of salvation history and in the micro level of our daily lives. However, this is not a one-way street. Worship also fuels memory. Whether we're pondering the goodness of God while doing the washing up, expressing our love for him by our actions or singing words of worship in a church service, we are worshipping with our lives. Our lifestyles and worship-words, attuned to the Spirit, help remind us of who we are and who God is.

Gathered and Scattered Lives

We worship God as individuals, in both lifestyle and in specific times of conscious praise and prayer. It's important to come to God as we are, to honour him when no one is watching and to listen to him, recognising the nudgings of the Spirit in our lives. We are also called to reflect on the nature of worship, not confining it to songs or liturgies on a Sunday but making it a vein running through every action in our lives. In every moment there is the potential to worship.

Corporate worship also aids our remembering. We share experience and remind each other what it means to worship and who it is we are worshipping. Testimony is a powerful factor in gathered worship: sharing thoughts and lessons learned and revisiting memories. In our calling to remember God, we are not alone. We celebrate God's goodness together; we also engage in corporate lament. As a body, when one part suffers we all suffer. This is – or should be – reflected in our corporate worship, reminding us of who we are as the body of Christ. If we separate ourselves from the body, we are isolated. This will be truer for some than for others, depending on their personality; nevertheless, even for those who prefer solitude, contact with others – in whatever form – nurtures our remembering faith and provides us with more opportunities to re-enact our story.

We help each other in our remembering and by doing so reinforce our potential for change. Our faith journeys interweave with those around us. We encourage each other by sharing and re-sharing the memory of God in our lives. We can pray for each other continually, asking that we may inhabit a state of remembering where God is present at the front of our minds, not shuffled to the back.

The Propagation of Memory

How important are the words we use in our worship, whether in private prayers of praise or public songs and liturgies? What are we saying in these moments – is it helpful and true? Are we focusing on our ideas of what we think God should be, rather than who God is? What we say in our lyrics and our liturgies is embedded in us, more than we often realise. What are we embedding? Without discernment, we can hold sincere beliefs, but beliefs that are actually a distortion of reality, or at least very limited interpretations of it.

The way we worship is an important aspect in helping us remember our Christ-identities. This can be through rhythm and pattern – song words storing themselves in different parts of our brains (so that if age and illness steal our memories we can still access these words). It might be in the way we act towards others – embedding new behaviours and new priorities, showing the light of God to the world and experiencing the wonder of the Holy Spirit working through us.

We cannot help but be subjective. Genuine objectivity is extremely hard to come by, if not impossible! We are all subject to influence from own experiences, culture, personality, genes, and memories. What beliefs have we collected along the way? How did we come by them? What is our authority, and are we interpreting that authority correctly?

So many questions and if we're not careful, they can tie us in knots so that we distrust everything. We need a gentle, discerning approach, asking God's Spirit to guide us in how we interpret experience, tradition and Scripture. Worship helps us remember, giving us pegs on which to hang our thinking, even if these are single words: Saviour. Maker. Friend. Constant triggers are required to keep our memories fresh and to inspire us in our daily living.

Words have limitations. I can rehearse the story of my faith repeatedly, but if I've not taken the time to understand it, explore it, and ask *why* I believe it, my response to any question will be half-hearted, inauthentic, even defensive.

The Power of the Back Story

When I've read advice on how to write a novel, I've come across those who advocate writing exhaustive profiles for all their characters – not just their personalities and the colour of their eyes but their histories, all that has happened to them and formed them. Mini-biographies, as it were, containing a lot of information that doesn't appear in the novel itself.

My initial reaction was that this seemed like a lot of extra work! Perhaps I need to rethink my response, if I really care about the story. By doing this the author *knows* his/her characters, understands them deeply and senses how they would react in certain situations. The characters' motivation is clear to the author, even if it's only gradually – or partly – revealed to the reader. For the reader, the characters seem more real because of the author's endeavour, even if they never know the full back story.

Research of place and culture has a similar role: writers may learn many things which never appear in their stories and yet these things become embedded in them. The author's voice is more authentic because of it.

So, too, with faith.

Often we don't take time to consider our back stories, to indulge in the tangents of our own minds, to allow ourselves to seek God in new ways, making new stories to remember. We may not include these in potted testimonies or even feel able to put them into words, but if we have embedded the God-story into our hearts it will radiate between the lines. Our faith is more authentic because of it.

A Whole New Landscape

Who is my neighbour in an increasingly globalised culture? Those who witness our lives, in both word and in action, are no longer just the people we see every day but those we encounter online. Many of us are busy sharing our thoughts, opinions and often our feelings with an array of people we've never – or at least rarely – 'physically' met.

How does this impact our witness? There is a whole new landscape out there, so what will be the nature of our contribution to it, our 'digital footprint', if you like? Do we use these new arenas to encourage, to build one another up and to challenge injustice? Or do we use them to gripe and to grumble, to puff ourselves up in the face of this new audience? If witness and worship are part of how we choose to live, then this area should be no different. However, people often apply different rules, even if not consciously. We've found a stage for our opinions, a place where we can complain or, let's face it, be unkind.

The wider the landscape of our lives, the more likely we are to come across opposition to our own worldviews. This opposition is not always polite. The challenge is: do we remember our identity and calling? Do we remember to act with grace? Or do we find ourselves typing words we'd never say to someone's face? It's so easy to forget that behind the words on the screen is an all-too-vulnerable person, and that our behaviour towards them may have a profound impact on them, for better or worse.

Have we found an outlet for all the unkind bits within ourselves, or do we see this as an opportunity to 'do' grace – proper, stunning, unrelenting grace? Do we turn the other cheek in the digital arena, when barbed retorts can flow so fast? Do we embrace the call to love when love seems impossible, even inexcusable?

It was Jesus himself who went beyond the command to love our neighbours, calling us to love our enemies too.

The Smiley Face of Grace

Always be ready to make your defence to anyone who demands from you an account of the hope that is in you; yet do it with gentleness and reverence. Keep your conscience clear, so that, when you are maligned, those who abuse you for your good conduct in Christ may be put to shame.

1 Peter 3:15b–16

Grace has the power to shape a conversation. I once had an intriguing Twitter exchange with an atheist who was convinced I was delusional and that religion was the root of evil. I didn't rise to his comments and the conversation progressed. I asked questions; he replied. I challenged him; he challenged me. We even thanked each other for being respectful. 'I still think you're wrong,' he said at the end. But in one of his last tweets he added a smiley face. That little emoticon indicated that it was indeed a gracious disagreement. Even if he thought I was deluded. Even if I thought him misinformed. Even if neither of us changed our minds.

So often we battle to be admitted right by a perceived opponent. I would suggest that the first battle is within – challenging ourselves not to respond in kind, to speak with grace rather than thinking up our most clever and laudable retort. Our witness is not just about what we say, but how we say it. If *that* battle is won, there is far more space and opportunity for us to explain ourselves. Perhaps they may listen more than we realise.

We are gracious not because of what grace achieves; that invalidates the nature of grace. Grace is itself the reason: remembering what has been done for us, remembering who we are called to be, even if we are ridiculed in the attempt. We may disagree with our whole hearts. In spite of this, by expressing ourselves graciously we are saying something about the faith we proclaim. That's the calling of grace. It's tough, but it's powerful.

Ironically, if we're unsure of our beliefs we often end up more defensive of them, not less. We want to smooth over our doubts and brace ourselves for apparent attack. How can we move beyond anxious defensiveness and inhabit the place of gracious believing – and behaving?

Symbiosis

The recollection and repetition of our stories is part of our worship and essential to our witness. If we cease to remember key aspects of our salvation story, our worship can get misplaced and our witness become empty. We aren't equipped to respond to others' questions as we've forgotten the answers ourselves.

We can only give an authentic response to a questioner if we are seeking God for ourselves, desiring a deeper understanding of the truth of his gospel. Because when questioners diverge from the script, we can feel like a telemarketer with a list of prepared responses. We scramble for the right thing to say and panic when it is not evident.

To remember God is to allow the knowledge of God to be embedded in us, so that even if we have no easy answer (and there may be none), we can respond in a way that demonstrates our relationship with him. We rely not on ourselves but on the prompting of the Holy Spirit. We act out the gospel in the way we behave.

Everything is interconnected. When we put it all in separate boxes, no wonder we struggle. Worship and witness are interdependent in our lives, feeding and informing each other. One without the other becomes weak. Worship is not just for Sundays. It's for every day.

> If I claim to worship a God of justice, but do not act justly in my own life, what kind of worship (or witness) is that?
> If I talk about a God worthy of our worship but rarely take the time to worship him, what kind of witness (or worship) is that?
> And if I remember God only in the abstract, with no impact on either worship or witness and no input into my living, what kind of remembering is that?
> Not the kind God requires of me.

God does not need us to defend him to the world; he's far too big for that. But we are chosen to reflect God, to know God, to share God.

Dare I say it? To *remember* God in a distracted world.

Going Deeper

Sometimes we spend our lives splashing about in the shallows, never daring to kick out for the deep end. Our feet won't touch the bottom there; we have to rely on God to keep us afloat and he doesn't, not always, not in that immediate way we'd like.

Sometimes we need to struggle in the deep end in order to learn to swim, getting slowly stronger, shaking off unhelpful platitudes that only pull us further under and embracing authentic faith – a faith not afraid to question and to mourn, but also a faith determined to trust in the face of life in all its madness – not dependent on ever-changing circumstances but dependent on the never-changing God. Knowing that when all else fails, God is.

A *remembering* heart carries with it an appreciation of grace, a readiness to listen to the Spirit, and a humility able to confess that which it does not know. A remembering heart embodies witness; it does not have an 'evangelistic' mode whereby witness becomes something only for special occasions. Instead it *lives* its witness, unafraid of being misunderstood, because it is aware of something greater.

A remembering heart is a compassionate heart, a heart consumed by love and a passion for justice in equal measure. It echoes God's own heartbeat, for God is both the source and the focus of its remembering.

I long for a heart such as this.

> *O for a heart to praise my God,*
> *A heart from sin set free;*
> *A heart that always feels Thy blood*
> *So freely shed for me...*
> Charles Wesley (1707–88)

FOR REFLECTION

- What do worship and witness mean to you? Do you need to widen your definition? Where do you think they overlap?
- Do you feel threatened when someone questions your faith? Write down the feelings this creates. Try and identify any particular causes of your anxiety.
- In what ways is the Holy Spirit essential to both worship and witness?

Part IV
The Art of Remembering

Chapter 16
Ways to Remember

Great is the power of memory. It is a true marvel, O my God, a profound and infinite multiplicity! ... Behold in the numberless halls and caves, in the innumerable fields and dens and caverns of my memory, full without measure of numberless kinds of things ... I penetrate into them on this side and that as far as I can and yet there is nowhere any end.
St Augustine, *Confessions* 10.17.26

The Potency of Memory

Memory fascinates us. Long before scientists started trying to identify this mysterious process, novelists, poets and thinkers reflected on the power of memory. Augustine of Hippo was fascinated by memory, calling it the 'belly of the mind' (*Confessions* 14.21), where joy and sadness could both be found, just as the stomach contains both bitter and sweet foods. He marvelled at the unfathomable nature of seemingly endless memory.

In Greek mythology, memory was personified as the Titaness Mnemosyne, from which we get the word *mnemonic*.[40] Memory, like love and war, got its own god, its heroine of old. Throughout history, memory has often been placed on a pedestal, as a transformative, precious thing to pursue and improve.

In recent times our understanding of memory has shifted. Memory is no longer seen as a god, but as another muddled and fallible aspect of our lives. Nonetheless, it remains important to us, and we can still idolise it. It is the stuff our personal stories are made of, its potency fuelling our very identities, our relationships, our communities, and our sense of culture. It ties the threads between us and our world and builds our understanding of ourselves and of one another, telling us where we have come from and how we got

[40] A technique or device that aids remembering.

here. This is true from the individual memory of leaving the house this morning and the events of a childhood birthday party to the collective memory of the origins of our ancestors – stories passed down through families and communities.

Memory maintains our relationships and enshrines our stories. In an aging population we are often more fearful of losing our memories than we are of losing our lives. We do not want to forget what we believe. We do not want to forget who we love, or have them forget us. We do not want this degree of bereavement. Without memory, we feel anchorless, and yet so often we take it for granted. It is partly this 'taking for granted' that makes its loss so shocking. It is the art of the everyday and the any-day, days that build up our lives.

Do the expectations and pressures of our culture and environment cause us to forget, by filling our minds with other things? They can stifle our hearts' desires and our longing for a deeper understanding of God, shuffling them into a folder marked 'later'. One day we realise we never found that 'later' and never reopened those hopes and dreams. If the values emphasised around us are not the values of the God of the weak and the poor, of the orphan and the broken-hearted, how can we *remind* ourselves of these values?

A jolt of memory, a reminder, can carry pang after pang of grief and regret. *How could I possibly have forgotten?* We can dismiss these former hopes as naïve, unreasonable, empty dreaming. But deep within us, something mourns.

Faced with this, how can we learn the art of remembering? How can we once again value memory in a more conscious way, not just through fear of forgetting but by the pursuit and practice of remembering? Memorisation, once valued, is now deemed old-fashioned. But what happens when we rely on outside sources to act as our 'memory'? The intimate connections we make, that personal flavour, can be lost. Surely there is still a place for personal remembering, for retaining something of what we learn? So that, if left bereft of all other information sources, we would still *know* the things that are important?

Part of the art of remembering is distinguishing the important from the unimportant. We cannot absorb everything, so in order to accumulate and retain knowledge we need a large dose of wisdom and discernment.

Consider these questions:

- What do I profess to be the most important part of my life?
- Do I act as if it is?
- Am I right to value this above all things?

And one more: *How can I remember this?*

Knowing Me, Knowing You

Faith is a journey, with twists that can perplex, excite and grieve us. We all journey differently. We have diverse experiences, genetic tendencies, inbuilt personality types, all of which inform us and make us who we are. We may be extrovert or introvert. Our natural inclinations mean that we draw our energy from different places – be it from time alone, chatting over coffee, or amid a gaggle of people. Understanding these things about ourselves helps us to give time to the parts of our lives which most nourish us, and in doing so, nurture our ability for deep-down remembering.

These days it's not a secret that people learn differently. Whatever categories you care to use, be it visual or linguistic, reflective or analytical, we have different ways of approaching information, of ingesting and digesting knowledge. This has been acknowledged in our churches, as people engage with different ways of exploring and presenting the gospel, not just through classic teaching models but through image, movement and informal discussion. Some respond well to such things, others do not – it takes them well out of their comfort zone because it is not their style, habit or preference.

If we have different styles of learning, isn't it reasonable to suggest that we have different ways of remembering? Remembering is how we recall what we have learned, how we revise and revisit it. How we learn and interact with the world surrounding us will naturally affect how we remember.

In the Old Testament, the people of Israel developed different ways of learning and remembering. Naturally their culture (like ours) had its own tendencies, its own 'trends', if you like. But the ways of remembering we see in the Old Testament laws and narratives are intriguingly diverse. They remembered by words – the written word, the Law and through the re-telling and listening to their identity-building stories. Within this there are further subcategories: recitation, memorisation and meditation, for example. Their lives and rituals were also filled with the visual and spatial – in the colour of the fabrics within the tabernacle and then the temple, the clothes the priests wore, the different emblems and memorials. All was heavy with *symbol*, brilliant for those who learned (and remembered) *visually*. Even the symbolism of the ceremonial laws (such as not wearing mixed fabrics) was a visual reminder of their calling.

Enacting Memory

Their lives were peppered with active remembering, in which they enacted events to remind themselves (and their children) of past events. The various festivals are good examples – such as the festival of booths, where they all lived in tents for a week to remember the Israelites' wilderness living. This style of dramatic enactment was intrinsic to how they conducted their feasting and their fasting, not least in the Passover itself. Here they ate and acted in a way that enabled them to remember the events of that last night in Egypt, using words, image and motion – great for kinaesthetic learners[41] who experienced it by touching, tasting (bitter herbs) and other actions.

They celebrated through music and dancing. There were specific people allocated for those tasks, ensuring that God was praised and made known in all kinds of ways. Through word, image, music and movement they made their memories real – allowing future generations to participate in these past events. Their memories fuelled their worship, and their worship helped them remember.

It can be hard for us to appreciate the role of sacrifice. Even if we grasp the concept the visualisation of it can confuse and repel us. It was a bloody, messy business and most of us recoil from it in a world where we no longer witness the killing of animals on a regular basis (although we eat them every day). The people of Israel would have had a far more vivid understanding than we do – of death and life, of slaughter, of blood. These things make us wrinkle our noses; we are accustomed to getting our meat hygienically packaged from the supermarket.

Consider the impact of this on someone who learns visually.

[41] A kinaesthetic learner responds to movement and sensory stimuli (the word is derived from *kinesis*, meaning movement or motion).

This graphic image and action told them something about the serious nature of sin; that life-blood, something their law held precious, was required to atone for it, as well as being necessary to approach a holy God. The power of the atonement rituals at Yom Kippur[42] relied heavily on visual spatial imagery and deliberate action – the spilled blood of one goat, and the sending away of the other, carrying the sins of the people into the wilderness. It's a physical demonstration conducted with a specific purpose in mind. Words were not enough – other means, other styles of learning were necessary to drive the point home to the *whole* community.

Once for All

In the New Testament, the early church continued with some of the rhythms and motions of ancient Judaism, going into the temple to pray regularly, gathering together to sing and make music. Of course, much of the Old Testament ritual was superseded by what Jesus did. All other sacrifices were now unnecessary in his Once for All sacrifice, a sacrifice made by a High Priest who does not need to sacrifice himself over and over again.

However, the image of sacrifice was still vibrant in their culture. This powerful visual element was now applied to Jesus himself. But it is clear now that these are *only* images of reality, not reality itself, shadows and sketches of the real thing, embodied in what Christ did and still does for us.

In place of the old Passover came the meal of remembrance, the Last Supper, another meal where action was mirrored, imagery made plain in physical symbols, and words said in order to remember. Memorisation can be effective – be it of words or of actions. We still do it, even if unconsciously, through our liturgies and prayers, through our hymns and songs. For just as they did for those we read about in Scripture, our memories help us to worship, to serve and to follow the One who goes before us.

Rawness of experience makes metaphors come alive. It was raw experience that the Passover commemorated and that we too commemorate when we think of Jesus and his birth, life, death and resurrection. Do we empty our remembering words of their vividness? Can we encounter the loss and the wonder of it all, or do we shy away from it, wincing at the idea that God could get his hands so dirty?

[42] The annual Jewish Day of Atonement.

Sometimes we want to find cleaner solutions. We dislike ideas of blood and sacrifice, of sweat, tears and death. Some find it utterly insulting. But the cross has always been a scandal, an affront. God becoming human – such messy flesh – has made people want to underemphasise the sheer humanity of Jesus. God uses the scandalous, the insulting, and the messy to change the world. It's there in the words of the last supper: *this is my body, broken for you; this is my blood, shed for you.* These are fleshy reminders of the hope of our salvation, symbolised by ordinary and edible elements of bread and wine. We are to swallow them, ingest them, digest them, even! How's that for vivid, messy metaphors of remembering?

Help me remember, God –
remember you in all kinds of ways
find glimpses of you in both ordinary
and extraordinary,
recognise you are the God
of every place.
Help me know you better.

FOR REFLECTION

- What helps you in your journey with God? What hinders you?
- Think about the elements you enjoy in a church service. What does this tell you about how you learn and remember?
- How can you harness what you know about yourself in order to get to know God better?

Be Thou my vision, O Lord of my heart;
Naught be all else to me, save that Thou art
Thou my best thought, by day or by night,
Waking or sleeping, Thy presence my light.

Be Thou my wisdom, Thou my true word;
I ever with Thee, Thou with me, Lord;
Thou my great Father, I Thy true son;
Thou in me dwelling, and I with Thee one.

Be Thou my battle shield, sword for the fight;
Be Thou my dignity, Thou my delight;
Thou my soul's shelter, Thou my high tower:
Raise Thou me heavenward, O Power of my power.

Riches I heed not, nor man's empty praise,
Thou mine inheritance, now and always:
Thou and Thou only, first in my heart,
High King of Heaven, my treasure Thou art.

High King of Heaven, after victory won,
May I reach heaven's joys, O bright heaven's Sun!
Heart of my own heart, whatever befall,
Still be my vision, O Ruler of all.

Ancient Irish, translated by
Mary Elizabeth Byrne (1880–1931),
versified by Eleanor Henrietta Hull (1860–1935)

Chapter 17
Faith and Familiarity

Search me, O God, and know my heart;
test me and know my thoughts.
Psalm 139:23

It can be tempting to think we already know what we believe, and that we don't need to dig deeper. But if we are not brave enough to ask ourselves questions and search for deeper meaning, how can we deal with the questions of others? We feel fearful when confronted with such questions about our faith, sensing an inadequacy within ourselves. We feel responsible for the reputation of the church, even of God himself. We don't want to let the side down.

We can never answer every question. We are not all-knowing. We have been entrusted with a message, but this does not mean we understand everything completely or correctly. Faith admits where it *lacks* knowledge. Genuine wisdom perceives the gaps in knowledge and recognises the harm of smoothing them over, or exaggerating what we know in order to fill the gaps. It's not about being able to answer everything as if it were a quiz question. It's about being able to give a thoughtful response, born out of a *seeking* faith, i.e. one that seeks to know, but recognises its limitations.

Making Space for Knowing Our Faith
How can we remember what we have never learned? Frequently, we have avenues for learning but we neglect to use them. With all the distractions, memory makers and the tiredness we feel, do we simply not have the time or the space? Perhaps we cannot summon any enthusiasm.

It can feel hard to make space for knowing our faith. There are things we must do, things we can't *not* do. Any extra 'requirement' taxes our time. We live in a time-poor society. The question needs asking: what are we doing that is not necessary? Initially, in our busy lives, we want to reply – *nothing*. Everything is scheduled in for a reason. If I don't do that, it will all fall apart. If I can't do that, I won't be able to do this and that's not what I want for my life.

What if, through circumstances beyond your control, you suddenly *had* to tone down your life? A debilitating illness. A lack of money or resources. What would you choose to lose? (This does not mean all the things you enjoy. If you were ill, eliminating the stressful bits would be far more important.)

We're used to cutting corners. We do it in order to fit in more activity, to make room for one more thing. What about making room – *in order to make room*? Room to grow and to learn, room to rest.

As part of my management of CFS/ME, I underwent some group work with an Occupational Therapist. We were all given the same goal – to manage our fatigue, to train our bodies to recharge, to adapt our lifestyles. Some group members had lifestyles more flexible than others. Others initially said: 'But I can't do that!' One woman was both full-time worker and mother. *Are you mad? How can I find time to rest?* In cases like these, it became a matter of finding what people *could* do.

Ways of Adapting

We asked ourselves: where is that pocket of time we could use to close our eyes and encourage our bodies to recharge? How could we *adapt* what we did – and needed to do – so it enabled us to discover those pockets of time and opportunity?

We all needed different approaches as we all led different lives. No time to rest in the office? One member simply chose to go outside, and sit in her car with the seat back during her break. Another arranged it with his boss so that he could lie down in the allocated 'medical room' for half an hour. All these things entailed a degree of courage in the face of others; we all had to be prepared to look 'different', which can be quite a challenge for the self-conscious! I had to be prepared to walk in late to a church service as I'd been lying on the floor of my husband's office (the perks of a minister's wife?!).

Originally, the group all looked at our lifestyles and thought: *How? It's not possible!* However, forced by necessity, we found there were parts of our lives we could tweak. Use break times more effectively. Set the alarm earlier so we didn't feel rushed and stressed at the beginning of the day. Focus on relaxing at the end of the day, not being tempted to fill every last minute with *doing*. We had to sacrifice some of the things we had previously considered essentials. You know what? *It turned out they were only habits.*

Life may not be favourable but it can be adapted. If you want time to explore and reflect, to know and to grow your faith, it can be found. You may just need a different template. Your life will require different adjustments to that of another. We all have different demands, limitations and desires which we programme in to our days and weeks. We have to bear in mind our personality types and learning styles, too. Some things won't work for us, and that's fine.

'No' can be a horribly hard word to say. Saying no to others is bad enough. Saying no to yourself – that takes *real* practice. We can become so used to our activities and habits that it can feel daunting to set aside a 'pocket of time'. It feels threatening in its newness.

Our lives are full of habits: what we do to wind down, what we do to gear up. How we react to situations as they occur. How we speak to people. Our attitudes towards life. Our expectations of ourselves and of others. What we do when we feel happy, angry or depressed. Even our mannerisms are habits!

If pressed, we can usually identify (and reluctantly confess) the real time-swallowers in our lives. Addictions also come in – not necessarily drastic, flamboyant sorts but seemingly minor things. How much time do we spend on our computers, tablets or smartphones? What about emotional issues – how much time do we spend paralysed by fretfulness, burning with anger or feeling resentful? Do we spend most days worrying about the next one? Perhaps it is a more a question of how much *energy* we spend. Are we addicted to work, at the expense of rest and play? Are we perfectionists, always wanting to get *every detail right*, even the ones that don't really matter? These details can take away our time – and our time with others.

Busy Is the Thing to Be

As we've seen, stress itself can become an addiction. When we stop, we don't know what to do with ourselves. We are so accustomed to being busy that we are *scared* of the non-busy. Or, we idealise the concept of having 'space' or 'peace and quiet' but find it so difficult when we attempt it that disillusionment immediately kicks in and we give up.

'Keeping busy' becomes our main goal. Our brains tell us that this is the norm, and when we stop we get symptoms of withdrawal. We get stressed by the absence of stress! We are no longer happy to stay still. This is fuelled by the immediacy and variety of our media-heavy age. Our brains seek out busyness and entertainment, even in times of rest. Boredom is becoming more of an issue because we are used to constant stimuli.

Busyness makes us feel valuable, but is busyness biblical? The Bible praises diligence, true. However, diligence and busyness are not the same, at least not that frenetic 'must get it all done' busyness that we so often practise. Habitual diligence is good. But habitual busyness?

Another thing I had to work on during my Occupational Therapy programme was dealing with the desire to be a perfect finisher. In other words, I will not always be able to finish every job; I will need to leave things and come back to them. Some things will never be done as well as I would like them to be.

So often we aren't satisfied until we've finished. So why do we start so many things? One of the symptoms of our busy world is an urgent need to complete tasks, ticking them off as soon as we can. *But do we really want to live as if the world – as if life – was a tick list?*

Breaking the Habit

Habits are hard to break. We need to start small, find the most manageable thing and not be tempted to overdo it. This tiny moment of space may feel like a huge challenge, yet even when being climbed on by a toddler, pausing between tasks in the office or sitting in a busy waiting room, we can try and allow our thoughts to focus on God. This will be in a way that we, as individuals, find helpful – be it through running through a phrase in our heads, looking at an object or picture, or simply becoming aware of the rhythm of our breathing. It's not easy. We may not succeed, but we are beginning to try. How can it be worse to try than never to try at all?

If our faith is important to us, if *God* is important to us – isn't it important to try? Simply by working through a phrase such as praying 'Lord, have mercy', or focusing on a characteristic of God, we are reminding ourselves of a greater presence in our lives. We are choosing not to forget.

One reminder leads to another. We can expand these new

habits – both in time and in scope. Perhaps we could set ourselves the task of reading through a book of the Bible, even if we only manage a few verses a day. In fact, a slower, prayerful reading may make us notice things we never saw before. We are allowing ourselves a chance of *knowing our faith* better.

Understanding the ways we learn will help. Perhaps we learn and remember better by *listening*. There are lots of audio resources: podcasts, audio books, recorded talks or seminars. Perhaps we think more deeply when outside, taking a walk or sitting on a bench. What about wandering round an art gallery? Don't dismiss it because it feels like a luxury; be willing to try. Maybe it's reading a favourite poem or immersing ourselves in music – the kind we know will bring out the longing in our hearts. Perhaps we prefer scribbling in a journal, blogging or reading – all these things can be used to help open our minds to learning and remembering, forming those all-important connections that keep memory vibrant. Or maybe we learn better through *talking*, finding someone and somewhere we can discuss things over coffee or a meal, rediscovering the buzz of sharing thoughts or feelings, interacting with others.

Finding someone wise and trustworthy to talk to is a good idea. Not all people's thoughts will be helpful to us or our faith, so it's important to balance them with wise words. We need to make sure our support systems are in place, to recognise our kindred spirits and our mentors, those who genuinely care about us.

Testing, Testing

We need to test things. Do they help us or hinder us, feed us or starve us? We choose that which we know is beneficial and enables us to grow as disciples while, at the same time, being willing to try something different. What excites you and what bores you? Do you respond to language or pictures? Quiet rooms or busy coffee shops? Do the opportunities of social media inspire you or distract you?

Which senses engage you the best – and the worst? Do you like variety or do you prefer a very specific focus? What stimulates you – alone time or lots-of-people time? Think about how you can harness your strengths to learn about and remember your faith. Consider what it is that sparks your interest and makes you *want* to engage. Apply that realisation to your attempts at growing and learning in faith. Some people find it valuable to have a 'quiet time' but others find it a struggle. We can't apply a blanket template to so many personalities. By doing this we can make others feel like perpetual failures, unable to fit the accepted mould. Why should they? God made us *different*.

Don't feel confined by the idea that you should never question anything. Many learn best by asking questions. Jesus often used questions – responding to other people's questions with his own! Allow yourself time to question, to take note of the things that puzzle you or distress you and pray about them. Recognise wise and understanding people in your life (they are rarely those who claim to have all the answers!) and talk to them. Get to know people who are both similar and different from you and let yourself learn from both.

Don't hide your struggles due to embarrassment. We need to struggle in order to grow. Instead, hold them out before God and ask for wisdom. All the techniques we use for remembering are simply surface stuff; what we need is God's help underpinning and infusing our efforts with the Spirit's strength. There may be times when all we can manage is to pray for the desire to know and remember, before we even get to the actual knowing and remembering.

A Wise Heart

Wisdom is in constant movement, reacting to life around it. It interacts; it shares when appropriate. It takes time to understand what it claims about life and meaning. If we are unconvinced by our own faith, we will never have real courage to share it with those around us. By grounding ourselves in our faith while allowing the fluidity that comes from mystery, we discover a faith that listens as well as speaks. A dynamic faith, which remembers, recalls and reinvestigates continually. An interactive faith is less likely to suffer from forgetfulness, because it is constantly bringing things to mind. It constantly asks questions and revisits past experience, applying this to present and future realities. It forms a wise heart and a mind that is trained on Christ, focused on knowing Christ and listening to the Spirit.

An intelligent faith allows for uncertainty within the journey, continuously set on 'discovery' mode. At no point does it say 'no more information, please' or 'closed – all facts found'. Intelligent faith continually explores and ingests new information and old, forgotten information. But it is not swayed by every breeze and empty philosophy. It builds its certainty on the person it follows, not the path itself. It has the resources to consider everything wisely, to recognise that which is unhealthy and misleading, because intelligent faith is also *discerning* faith. It weighs up information and compares and contrasts it with what it has already discovered – slotting in the good and deflecting the unhealthy. Faith journeys by nature. It encompasses moments of both movement and stillness, travel and pause. It *grows*. Everywhere it travels it detects reminders. Things that cause it to recall and apply, things that carry associations.

> *Lord, give me a seeking heart,*
> *a hungry mind.*
> *Allow me what I need*
> *to refuel and re-flame.*
> *Give me release*
> *from dullness and mediocrity.*
> *Help me remember.*
> *Give me the wisdom*
> *to know what I need to do.*

FOR REFLECTION

- What do you have in your life that you consider a necessity? Is it?
- How can you adapt your life so that you feel healthier – spiritually, mentally and physically? Where are your potential 'pockets of time', however small?
- Consider those 'testing' questions you've found in this chapter. How would you respond?

Bless the Lord, O my soul,
and do not forget all his benefits—
who forgives all your iniquity,
who heals all your diseases,
who redeems your life from the Pit,
who crowns you with steadfast love and mercy,
who satisfies you with good as long as you live
so that your youth is renewed like the eagle's.
Psalm 103:2–5

Chapter 18
Methods of Memory

These things I remember,
as I pour out my soul:
how I went with the throng,
and led them in procession to the house of God,
with glad shouts and songs of thanksgiving,
a multitude keeping festival.
Psalm 42:4

A friend once gave me a necklace. When I pick it up to wear, I think of her and recall all our stories: shared confidences, embarrassing moments, how our friendship began. The association is that strong.

The Association Game
Our minds are wonderfully complex things, full of deep and personal connections. A noise can make you think of your childhood; a smell can remind you of past summers. Even a touch or taste can trigger something – if you once ate too much of a certain flavour, or got food poisoning from a certain ingredient, the memory alone can make you feel queasy at the taste of it (please don't feed me anything with tarragon in it!). Direct or indirect, pleasant or unpleasant, associations are everywhere.

The Israelites knew the power of association. It was there in their symbols and memorial stones. Reminders carry associations. A souvenir reminds you of a certain holiday. It may be because of how it looks – a picture or a model of some well-known place or monument, but associations go deeper than that. My husband remembers where he was when he bought his first CD. The CD itself gives nothing away on this score. He remembers not just the fact he owns that CD, but recalls the event of buying it.

The power of association is not just confined to objects

themselves but to places. We remember the experiences we had *in this place*. We have positive – or negative – memories whenever we walk down that street, or stand in that room. We remember joy and we remember pain. The stronger the feeling, the more dramatic the experience, the more deeply we relive it. Association leads to attachment – objects and places become important to us because of the associations they carry for us. Friends and family are special to us because we have come to know them, and have shared experiences with them.

These experiences and associations are not static. When we return to a place we once knew well, we return with all our new experiences in tow. Not only are there things that simply weren't there before – that shop has closed, that bench is new – but we come primed to notice things we didn't see before. Having had more life experience, we are interested in different things. As soon as we return, the memories begin to adapt, encoding the new into the old narrative.

Memory is fluid. Some would call this fallibility, and certainly we need discernment when approaching memory. But the inventiveness of the human mind is both strength and weakness – startling in its intensity, both dangerous and beautiful in its potential.

The Power of Place

Habits breed not just through actions but *where* those actions are performed. The power of association is something we can harness in our efforts to keep remembering, to practise training our minds and getting to know – or re-know – our faith.

Workplaces are a good example of association in action. For those who have a specific space for doing their work, it makes the tasks easier to focus on. Other distractions, other associations, are less likely to pull us away. In comparison, the discipline to use a multi-purpose space for working can be much harder to summon. For those who work from home, creating a 'space' to differentiate work activities from leisure and family is often important.

I write best when I'm out of the house – usually in a coffee shop. This removes the potential for doing anything else. I'm easily distracted at home. I've learned that by changing my location, I can focus and enjoy the process of writing. It's not always practical, but

I recognise the need for it wherever possible. By creating space for myself to write, I give myself a better chance at doing it well.

For some, such a space is desperately important. This is as true for their spiritual lives as for anything else. Some mark the moment with a sense of 'sacred space'. This may involve using a certain chair, or even turning a chair in a certain direction – to differentiate it from its other uses, with other associations. Even if we have to drag ourselves to a certain place, once we're in it, association kicks in and we can harness the power of habit.

Some fortunate people have an entire room that they use as a personal study or for quiet reflection. For most of us, this will not be the case. Our spaces and places are often overlapping, crammed with things, people, activity. We adapt, as we do in all things. We find a pocket of space.

Once again, each of us will be dealing with different issues. A period of self-examination is necessary to discover what needs working on in our lives, and the best *way* to work on it. There is no 'one size fits all', although there will be those styles and sizes we find helpful – as well as those we don't.

Memory Markers

We can experiment with our own memory techniques – *mnemonics,* to use the official word. These often use association in order to remember. Some create mental images to prevent them forgetting something – a person holding a certain item, wearing particular colours, sitting in a specific place. The more unusual the better, as it makes it more memorable. I struggle a little with doing this – imagining my husband sitting on the dining room table with a pumpkin on his head feels rather ... weird. But perhaps I should embrace the weirdness, if it helps me remember!

One technique is to try and super-impose an association onto a certain item. So whenever I look at the bottle of ketchup (or whatever item it is) it triggers the memory I want to recall. Sometimes it works; sometimes it doesn't.

Of course the kind of remembering I'm advocating in this book is not mere 'to do list' remembering. However, perhaps the method behind these techniques of remembering can still help us in our lives of faith. For example, remembering to spend time listening to God (although I don't propose imagining God with a pumpkin on his head). If we associate something with this act, whether it is an item or an action, looking at it or doing it can trigger a response – *ah, yes, I've not done that recently.*

Our ability and desire to acknowledge God can get swamped by other chores and pressures. If we've found a way to help us remember God, whatever way that may be, we can build on our spiritual remembering. By creating associations with certain images, items or actions, we can remind ourselves of our intentions – which can often get lost in the hurried muddledness of life.

God speaks to us in different ways, through words, people, places and pictures. By creating reminders of God communicating with us we help ourselves not to forget the depth and importance of what we have learned. A smooth pebble might sit on the table reminding us of a moment where we walked by a stream and felt God's presence with us. A postcard of a lighthouse might prompt us to remember an analogy which spoke to us about God's guidance in our lives. We are always doing this; that's what mementoes *are*, reminders of events or of people, things we deem precious because of what they signify – even if they would mean something entirely different to someone else.

Boxing Memories

We could keep 'memory boxes' – things that remind us of different points God has spoken to us, be it a verse from the Bible, a written account, an object symbolising a profound moment. By frequently opening this box of associations we rehearse those memories and keep them fresh. That way we do not come across something later and grieve, thinking *how could I have forgotten?* Instead we frequently re-celebrate the memory, strengthening old connections.

I have several shoe boxes which act in this way. I didn't set them up as memory boxes – they were merely ways of storing all those little bits and bobs I've accumulated, be it cards, pictures, event tickets, notes from friends, a poem someone gave me once, etc. However, even as they are they act as little memory treasure troves. Every now and then I'll go through one, pausing over item and allowing memories to resurface.

Pay Attention!

My child, be attentive to my words;
incline your ear to my sayings.
Do not let them escape from your sight;

keep them within your heart.
For they are life to those who find them,
and healing to all their flesh.
Proverbs 4:20–22

Association on its own is not enough. In order to remember something, we need to have paid attention to it in the first place. Paying attention helps us not only to remember accurately but to make those personal associations and attachments that help us remember.

As we've seen, our working memories can only hold a certain amount of things at one time. If this capacity is exceeded, a filter effect takes place. Some things are lost almost instantly. Therefore when I go from one room to the next thinking about several things, I can completely forget the purpose of going between rooms. The thing with the strongest hold on my attention will be the one I remember – distracting me from my original task.

An Age of Distraction?

Attentiveness is essential to remembering. It's the first action we can take against forgetfulness, but it's often under siege. This has always been the case, but we live in an age of distraction, so much tugging at our attention continually, crowding into our minds and crying out for us to look! Look! Look! Our brains are not adapted to the sheer volumes of information now at our disposal – 'information overload' is becoming a cliché, but clichés are often based in truth.

To some degree we get used to it, even becoming addicted to the constant stream of information on offer. We love the thrill of variety and the satisfaction of instant communication, of being in touch with a world far wider than our own. We like to click a button and get an immediate result. You could say we are habitually distracted; it becomes our default state. We need discipline in order to resist, but temptations are amply available.

This is not to say that the information age is a bad thing but, as with all cultural and environmental influences, it creates both benefits and problems. When we recognise that our brains are only equipped to attend to and remember certain amounts of information at one time, we see that 'information overload' is a problem we may need to address in our own lives.

Distraction has an opposite. What if we focus on the power

of attention, rather than the power of distraction? If we take this more positive angle, we can think about how to use the power of attention in our lives, recognising its importance in our efforts to remember.

This involves knowing our strengths and weaknesses. Are we easily distracted? We may need to take firmer measures. Even if we do not consider ourselves prone to distraction, it might be worth doing a kind of self-check to see if that is really the case and asking: how can I improve my attentiveness still further? How can I exercise it more frequently? Is my attention focused on the right place, object or person?

Changing Trains

I'm often distracted by things I need to do. They niggle away at the back of my mind, pulling my attention away from my current task and thus hampering my memory of it. My mind is full of tangents and side roads; I have to pull myself back so I don't lose my original train of thought. Absent-mindedness can lead to confusion and error, orange juice on your cereal instead of milk, finding a bag of partially frozen peas in the crockery cupboard (yes, that was me). Although these aren't major things, they demonstrate how distraction can muddle with our minds and memories. If our attention is pulled away at the wrong moment, it interferes with the memory-making process. Things get put in the wrong place.

Novelty is another lure. Many people find various communication technologies a constant tug at their attention and that is true for me too, but this tends to be more acute when I first start using it. When I first got a smartphone I was distracted by its mere presence – a door into so many worlds, so much communication – wanting to check continuously for updates and new messages. The novelty wore off, partly because I recognised it was distracting me. When we are unable, or unwilling, to recognise the things that distract us, we become more and more enslaved to them.

I typed the first draft of this in the library. It was so much easier than doing it at home, when my eyes and ears were tugged every which way, thinking I should be doing this or that, wondering what to prioritise, feeling guilty about the overflowing laundry basket. To the library I take my writing 'tools' and them alone, sitting and writing freed from distraction, experiencing the odd thrill of attentiveness while still being aware of the discipline it requires. It helps me think more clearly, learn more thoroughly and retain information better. By removing distraction and choosing to pay attention, I am laying the basis of memory. We need the twin methods of attention and association to help us focus, work and remember.

Let my thoughts dwell on you, O God
through the touchstones of my life.
May your Spirit infuse every moment,
breathing meaning into my experiences,
my struggles, my chores.
Meet me there.

FOR REFLECTION
- What holds strong associations for you? Why is this?
- Now list the elements in life that you find most distracting (remember these aren't necessarily 'bad' in themselves).
- What reminders do you keep of how God has worked in your life? Could you make your own memory box, or start a journal, for this purpose? Note down any ideas you have.

I will recount the gracious deeds of the LORD,
the praiseworthy acts of the LORD,
because of all that the LORD has done for us,
and the great favour to the house of Israel
that he has shown them according to his mercy,
according to the abundance of his steadfast love.
Isaiah 63:7

Chapter 19
Rhythms of Living

It is what we do routinely, not what we do rarely, that delineates the character of a person. It is what we believe in the heart of us that determines what we do daily.
Joan Chittister[43]

What and who we are is reflected in the manner of our daily living. Never underestimate the power of repetition. Even when we do not fully understand what we are repeating, something within us learns from it, ingests it and incorporates it into our understanding of life. Whether it is through action or word, what we repeat has power.

A Routine Existence?

Even if we find the concept of routines uninspiring, we all have them in some degree – ways of behaving, waking or sleeping, posture and preference, people and places. Life has rhythm. We exist in cycles of night and day, seasons of winter to spring to summer to autumn and back again, each living thing in a constant cycle of living and dying as existing cells are replaced by the new and as we grow from young to old.

Our routines reveal something about us. Sometimes they say things we might disagree with – suggesting that certain things are important to us and others are not. Looking at our lives and what we do with them – how we use our time – can be frightening. We find that the things we prioritise are not the things we consider the most important. What we *say* about our priorities and what we actually prioritise can be alarmingly different.

Routine is a natural reminder. We remember to do something because we have always done it. Thus the question is raised – is this something I need or want to remember to do? Or are we merely

[43] Joan Chittister, *The Liturgical Year: The Spiralling Adventure of the Spiritual Life* (Thomas Nelson, Nashville 2009), p. 183.

enslaved to habits, be they downright bad or merely mediocre, stealing time and energy from what we claim to be most important to us? Do we need to transform or even eradicate certain routines and put something healthier and more constructive in its place?

Most of us know when we've been wasting our time or energy. We feel sapped or depressed. We get irritated and frustrated with ourselves and may feel inclined to take this out on everyone else. We may not even realise we're doing it. We feel a sense of profound dissatisfaction, a sense of having achieved nothing. Now, this can be down to our feelings and may not be true at all – we can't always know the effect of our actions.

However, sometimes we fritter away our time because we have got ourselves into unhelpful rhythms, into lacklustre routines which drain us instead of energise us. We forget how to use the time we have. We forget how to *rest*, deeply and properly, when time becomes available. We forget to make time for resting. We can be tempted to think we are resting when in fact all we are doing is being distracted by different kinds of busyness, and wonder why we are still so tired at the end of it. We become programmed into certain ways of living.

Routine Reactions

Do not be conformed to this world, but be transformed by the renewing of your minds, so that you may discern what the will of God is – what is good and acceptable and perfect.

Romans 12:2

This is true of our thoughts, too. We can become so 'routine' in having negative thoughts about ourselves and those around us that it becomes a reflex reaction. We become *characteristically* self-destructive or unkind in our hearts. We call ourselves names, describe others derogatively, promote patterns of thinking that get set on the repeat cycle – to our detriment and to the detriment of our relationships. We are not remembering the reality of all that God has done for us; we are reliving what we have learned to think (wrongly) about ourselves. The script we live by is not written by God and his will for us, but by the sum of our disappointments, what we see as our 'failures' or poor choices.

We can learn a great deal from personal experience, but if we read from that experience using only our own smeared glasses, we get a distorted view. We are defined by who we are in Christ, who has set us free from these destructive patterns of thinking. Let's not program them in again.

If I fail to take regular stock of my life, I fall into unhelpful ways of thinking. I promote an understanding of myself that belittles me and God's purpose for me, and am tempted to 'beat myself up' for getting my focus all wrong. But we don't need to live our lives on a guilt trip, constantly queasy about everything and nothing. That's not what we were made for. The stories in Scripture tell of the frequent stumbling and mistakes of God's people – but he never gave up on them. A new start is always offered daily, even hourly. Do not focus on what has been lost; celebrate that God is never foiled by your circumstances. If we say repeatedly to ourselves 'I can't', perhaps we need to add 'but God can'.

Basing our patterns of remembering purely on ourselves makes us very introspective. In the Psalms, the writers often explain their circumstances and then call on their memories – not memories based purely on themselves and their own strength but memories of God's former actions, justice and mercy, of God's faithfulness and bigger story.

Plastic Brains

So why do we find it so hard to break and form habits of routine and rhythm? After years of believing that the adult brain does not change, it is now accepted that all our brains have a degree of plasticity. It may not be as easily changed as it is when we are children, but our brains still have astonishing abilities to change and adapt. When we experience activity, whether doing or simply thinking about something, our synaptic connections respond and adapt. When we repeat these actions and thoughts, we fire up the same synapses. Our brains even begin to *physically change shape* in relation to how we live our lives. One of the most famous examples is the study of London cab drivers, where the hippocampus of their brains was found to be enlarged due to the need for them to navigate and remember the vast network of London's roads.

When we form habits, we may be changing the shape of our brains! No wonder it feels difficult to break these habits; we have learned to think and behave in this way – a very literal learning. Yes, it's all 'inside our heads', but it is very real.

Two things occurred to me as I was thinking about this topic.

1. *There is hope!* We can still change. We do not have to say 'This is how I will always be'. It's not true that our brains are 'set' into one mould after childhood.

2. Our brains can change in both *negative* and *positive* ways. When we set ourselves to learn a good habit, we know that with work we can adapt to it. But the same is true of bad habits. If the way I think and live literally changes the shape of my brain it gives me pause. If I neglect to use certain circuits in my brain, they are weakened, and can eventually disappear altogether. This is brain-deep forgetting.

We already 'knew' in an abstract sense that practising something makes you better at it; that has been received wisdom for centuries. Now, there is new insight into the *mechanics* of the matter. As Nicholas Carr puts it in his book *The Shallows*, our brains are plastic, not elastic.[44] We can't just twang back into the previous shape. The longer practised and the firmer the change has been, the harder it is to change back or move into a new 'shape' (forgive my amateur descriptions here). Carr's fascinating book looks at the effect the internet is having on the way we think. He talks about how hard it is to discipline ourselves to read and focus as we used to, when now we are constantly zipping about consuming an enormous variety of information snippets. We learn to scan and skim everything, and that starts feeling like the natural way of doing things, 'second nature', you might say. Actually, our brains prefer it. It's not just an abstract thing but a real, physical change. Once our brains have adjusted and adapted to new ways of thinking and processing, it's hard *not* to do it this way. The old ways recede in the face of the new and the more obvious. It begs the question: what have I neglected? What good things about myself have faded away due to disuse? What other, less helpful things have I dwelled on and allowed to shape myself and my future?

Patterns of Forgetfulness

Is it possible our brains are accustomed to forgetting? Did the ancient Israelites create patterns of idolatry, their old habits sticking so hard because their brains had been programmed this way, not just by culture but by habit? Was the calling to worship *one* God –

44 See Nicholas Carr, *The Shallows: How the Internet Is Changing the Way We Read, Think and Remember* (Atlantic Books, 2010), pp. 34–35.

Yahweh – a challenge because their brains had somehow adapted to polytheism? This is just wild hypothesising on my part. But isn't it interesting to consider the possibilities, as we find out more about how our brains work? That the ideas of rhythms and routines, having been practised and reflected upon for centuries, have an effect on our brains, changing them – presumably for better or for worse. It's a little frightening. What is it that we do to ourselves when we start forming bad or unhelpful habits? It's also exciting – imagine the possibilities of what our brains can do, that we do not have to settle for what we have always been, that through the Spirit's transforming power we can *change*.

Forming New Rhythms

My soul is satisfied as with a rich feast
and my mouth praises you with joyful lips
when I think of you on my bed,
and meditate on you in the watches of the night;
for you have been my help,
and in the shadow of your wings I sing for joy.
Psalm 63:5–7

This is the strength of ancient spiritual practices that tap into ideas of rhythm and repetition. 'Routine' for many is a dull concept, and we can certainly end up on auto-pilot without reflecting on what we're doing. But chucking out the concept of routine may not be the best approach. Perhaps we need to re-imagine it, understanding that we all have different ways of remembering and not expecting every method or practice to work for everyone. But that doesn't mean we can't adapt this idea of a regular rhythm in our own lives.

By nature I am erratic, and easily bored. My routine needs to be something that sparks me off – and needs regular reshaping. But not *eradicating*.

You could see this routine-forming as something that requires stages in order to truly work – first *implementing* the routine, then regularly *reflecting* on it (so it doesn't lose its meaning), *applying* what you learn from it to other parts of life, and *reshaping* it when it starts losing its lustre.

Patterns are powerful things. A person suffering from a dementia-type illness may not know who's talking, but can still recite the Lord's Prayer perfectly, or recall a familiar hymn when prompted, because they're using a different part of their brains. I ask myself – if my memories get muddled, what patterns would I like to be able to recall? If my faith defines me, I want to infuse my memory with it in any way I can, so that I do not lose that which is most precious to me – knowing the God who loves me.

The Power of Practice

Whatever we are not using becomes underdeveloped. I often wish I was able to retain and grasp knowledge more effectively, able to make connections immediately – understanding issues, concepts, problems and their resolutions with high and speedy efficiency. As, alas, I am the sort who perpetually loses her thread and easily forgets what she has learned, that particular goal may be out of reach!

But I can try exercising. I may not be able to indulge in much weight-lifting initially, but that's because my muscles aren't trained for it. I'll never be a world-class weight lifter (either metaphorically or literally) but I can exercise and tone my mental muscles in order to stretch my mind and introduce more complex ideas. I can graduate from the milk to the solid food.

What if, in my pockets of time and of space, I stretch myself and start trying to lift 'heavier' objects? Initially it feels impossible. I could say – *This isn't me. I'll leave it to those who understand such things.* But then I underestimate myself and the natural abilities God has given me. I underestimate the plasticity of my brain. And I never get to see for myself the journey from A to B, or form my own conclusions. I am always relying on the conclusions of others, and have not practised enough to able to critique them constructively, to have the freedom to agree or disagree, to discern what is healthy and what is not, to know how to form the questions that frequently meddle with my mind.

Initially when learning a new subject or skill, or adapting to a new job, we can't imagine ever fully grasping it. We have to learn, to train ourselves, to *practise*. As we become familiar with things, we can introduce new skills, new responsibilities. As we learn more about something, it becomes easier for us to build on that learning. What we thought we would never be able to remember becomes part of our daily lives.

We do not need to stay with the familiar. In our spiritual lives we often forget to stretch ourselves in this way, not grasping our own capabilities to learn, grow and be transformed. Not grasping that we have the *ultimate* personal trainer: the Holy Spirit alongside us, spurring us on. Life requires movement, otherwise we grow stagnant; we feel lifeless and our minds seem mediocre. We wonder where we went wrong. We ask, privately, 'Surely there is more to life than this?'

Giver of life, train my heart to chase after you.

FOR REFLECTION

- What do you most want to change about yourself?
- What routines or spiritual disciplines do you already practise? Reflect on whether they work, and why.
- What new patterns and rhythms could you introduce, so that the 'important stuff' is more immediately memorable?

Now may our Lord Jesus Christ himself and God our Father,
who loved us and through grace gave us eternal comfort
and good hope, comfort your hearts and strengthen them
in every good work and word.
2 Thessalonians 2:16–17

Chapter 20
Recognising Grace

The grace of the Lord Jesus Christ, the love of God, and the
communion of the Holy Spirit be with all of you.
2 Corinthians 13:13

We all have special memories that we hate the idea of forgetting – they are precious, treasured things. We need to earmark the important memories and rehearse them so that we can still recall them later – to inhabit them, so that they propel us into better ways of living. This is the power of positive remembering: taking care to recall moments of revelation and gestures of kindness, *noticing* when someone has given us so much of their energy and time, not forgetting the blessings we have received. Some things it would be thoughtless to forget – unkind, even.

Many of us will know the pain of belated remembering, the pang we experience when we realise we never wrote that grateful email or acknowledged a loving gesture from another. The person at 'the other end' feels hurt and unacknowledged. Our intentions (even the very best of them) get swept away sometimes, and we succumb to a tragic form of amnesia whereby the love of others remains unacknowledged in our lives.

What then, of God? Of Jesus Christ on the cross? If we forget this ultimate act of loving kindness, of extraordinary grace, what honour do we give him? Gratitude is the only thing we have to give, but we often neglect to give it. We are no longer mindful of the God who has delivered us, just as Israel forgot God's saving acts in Egypt and his provision in the wilderness. We forget God's salvation and provision – we take it for granted and no longer call it to mind on a regular basis. Our songs and prayers become empty as we cease to remember what has been done for us.

God in My Living

I believe we need to start nurturing an awareness of God, through attentiveness and association, rhythm and routine, but also in the ordinary moments, free from obvious triggers and reminders. By learning to notice things – to register beauty, to respond to a smile – we slip out of the grip of the unhelpful memory makers such as worry, stress and fear. We allow ourselves to inhabit the present, and by doing so help ourselves come to a present awareness of God in our lives.

By allowing ourselves space to reflect on what we learn and remember, we harness the power of contemplative thinking. We make connections, apply them to our lives, grasp new significance and enliven our minds and memories. The more we remember, the more we *can* remember. Reflection allows memories to be both consolidated and recalled, promoting a sense of mindfulness. It gives us space to listen to the Spirit when the world gets so busy and noisy.

In many ways, mindfulness is an antidote to forgetfulness. It observes; it recalls; it remembers. We need to allow our minds to settle on a topic and not just ingest but digest it, forming an awareness of the subject so that when we move into another activity we are still 'percolating' at a subconscious level. We drip feed our memories, rather than overwhelm them, and by doing so make them last.

The concept of mindfulness is becoming very popular – a sense of awareness of the present, and of yourself within it, making no judgements, simply *feeling* – being *aware*. I'd like to put a different spin on this and say I want to become mindful not so much of myself and where I am but of God and what he is doing in my life. To allow myself to stop and listen, coming without presumption or expectation, simply developing a God-awareness in my life. Please note this is not an achievement, simply an item on my wish list! But increasingly I wonder if part of the antidote to my forgetful heart is to nurture a continual awareness of God – not by reserving it for a certain time of day but by making it the default setting of my heart. But how?

Collective Remembering

… encourage one another and build up each other, as indeed you are doing.

1 Thessalonians 5:11

We are called to togetherness. We are a body – a complete body not with a separate arm and a separate leg but one body with Christ as head. Living as the body of Christ has its challenges, its difficulties, its pains, but it is deeply important in our lives of remembering God. When we forget, our brothers and sisters are there to remind us – to remind us of the Big Story but also of the impact that has on our smaller stories.

We remind *each other* of God's presence. We don't rely on one person to do the reminding. We are community. We are family. If it's all about listening to one person something is askew – unless, of course, that person is Christ. Paul cried out against the factions in the early church; we belong to Christ, not to the most compelling leader or teacher among us![45]

If we neglect to help one another, the whole body suffers. We need each other in order to remember, to recognise the workings of grace in our lives. Through Christ and his indwelling Spirit, we support one another in a way that aids our remembering and nurtures an awareness of God.

Celebrating Memory

Rejoice always...

1 Thessalonians 5:16

We've been talking about memory in a way that implies need, duty, or importance. We need to remember. We should remember. But in all of this, memory is no less a gift. It is an extraordinary privilege to be able to recall and re-experience that which has come before us – and to participate in memories that originate beyond ourselves.

Memory is to be celebrated. We often do this unawares – meeting with friends and family, enjoying reminiscing together, reliving past shared moments, and experiencing the delight of recovering a memory. This can be a simple filling in of detail, a reminder of an entertaining moment, but it can also be more profound. A trigger in conversation can dig out a memory you had previously forgotten – even if it is just a flashbulb moment – an image of being with someone special, now gone. This new memory is something to treasure. You thought you had assembled all the pieces in your mind but no – here is another reminder, something unanticipated. Something for which you feel incredibly grateful.

Memory is so intrinsic to us that, as with so many things that

[45] See 1 Corinthians 1:10–17.

structure our lives, we take it for granted. It is when we are faced with the loss of it that we realise its importance to us. But rather than focusing on the idea of lack, why not look at what it gives us? Could consciously celebrating memory be a way of helping us remember better? The celebration of memory often involves a kind of dialogue, be it writing something down for our own benefit or in conversation with others. It's also part of our worship.

Memories shared are memories celebrated. Whether relating them for the first time and thus giving a new friend an insight into ourselves – our life stories, what is important to us, what entertains us; or sharing with someone who remembers the same thing – in their own unique way. With the addition of their perspective, the memory becomes more vibrant, more colourful. We learn to cultivate an attitude of rejoicing: look what has been done for us!

The Heart-cry

… pray without ceasing…

1 Thessalonians 5:17

Prayer helps us to nurture an awareness of God, and please note I'm not advocating a certain template of how we go about prayer. Prayer is our heart-cry to the God who loves us. It is our way of remembering him, constantly, in every jot and tittle of our lives. I think we get in such a muddle sometimes over how we should pray. We anticipate that God will react like those who criticise or condemn us. But in our moments of personal prayer, we don't need to worry – we just need to speak (not necessarily with words, or perhaps using someone else's words) to our heavenly parent, coming with all the flotsam and jetsam of our lives, laying it all – our hopes, our fears, our love – before God.

Prayer is relational. I've often heard people say, 'I'm not very good at praying'. Sometimes they mean they find it hard to pray full stop. Sometimes they simply feel their prayers are inadequate. God does not rate our prayers in terms of adequacy. We are called into *relationship* – dynamic, living relationship. Do we really believe that God acts as a kind of cosmic proofreader when we pray – noting all our stumbling pauses and raising his eyebrows at grammatical errors and poor descriptions? Do we *really* believe that this is what the God of grace is like? Our God, who sees the heart, whose very Spirit intercedes for us when we cannot find the words?

The act of prayer is both an act of remembering and a means of remembering. Without prayer, we are spiritually weak. Our faith-remembering is hampered; our thoughts of God shift further and further away. But how little I pray! And how deep is the contrast between my life and the call to 'pray without ceasing'.

Perhaps I have constricted my ideas of prayer. Perhaps I need to learn that sensitivity to God is a valuable part of my prayer life, a part in which the Spirit can groan the words I can't find or can't bring myself to say. I need to open myself to this Spirit, who alerts me to the fingerprints of God in this world and in my life. I need to acknowledge God in every moment: moments of grief and confusion, moments of delight and of thankfulness.

The Tonic of Thankfulness

... give thanks in all circumstances; for this is the will of God in Christ Jesus for you.

1 Thessalonians 5:18

We forget to be thankful. We consign it to an emotion, as we do 'love', so that thankfulness only occurs when we feel like it. But thankfulness, like love, is a choice. It is not about being dishonest; I need to admit when thankfulness is the last thing on my mind! But if I don't at least acknowledge its absence I am missing something – I am *lacking* – I am *forgetting*.

When we forget, we close our eyes to wider perspectives and get angered by the trivial irritations of life. We look down at our feet rather than looking to our Saviour. Forgetfulness has the astonishing ability to cast aside the miraculous, the testimony of the past, the faithfulness of God and carry on as if these had never occurred. It never sees the need for gratitude.

Forgetfulness forgets grace when the road ahead looks rocky. It forgets grace when relationships are struggling and says there are no ways of mending them. It forgets grace when it passes over the wounded, for fear of dirtying hands. It forgets grace every morning if we let it.

We forget the reality of what God has done. We doubt that he will care for us in the future. We forget that God has saved us and given us new clothes of dazzling white, and crowned us as co-heirs with Christ. In our forgetfulness we starve ourselves of the joy of his salvation, and wonder why we are hungry in our hearts.

Thankfulness, however, remembers. A remembering heart is a thankful heart. Thankfulness is nurtured by an awareness of God in our lives, and motivates us to seek God's purposes, loving and trusting God in everything. This is reflected in our behaviour and the way we treat each other. True thankfulness leaves no room for the endless struggle for acceptance. Thankfulness exists because we are already accepted. It is the truest, most real response to grace. It is not forced or begrudging; it is open-eyed to what has been done for us. We can't leave thankfulness behind. It is a result of remembering what God has done, and one of the ways in which remembering inspires worship and fuels witness. It gives us cause for rejoicing, it encourages us to pray. Together, we can spur each other on, growing into the people we were made to be.

Spirit-led Living

Do not quench the Spirit.

2 Thessalonians 5:19

The Holy Spirit is essential in our lives and in our remembering. It is the person of the Spirit who gives us strength for the journey, grace in the face of gracelessness, a deeper awareness of God and the things of God.

We cannot be Christ-like without this Spirit, because Jesus himself modelled an intensely full relationship with the Spirit – who anoints, empowers and instructs. Jesus embodied a Spirit-led life, and sent this helper to us, so that we too can be Spirit-led.

If we want to nurture an awareness of God and cultivate a remembering heart, we need the Holy Spirit of God. We need to be receptive to the Spirit stirring us. We need to recognise where the Spirit is working, to be discerning. To recognise the grace of God in our lives and demonstrate it to others.

Being Grace Bearers

The grace of our Lord Jesus Christ be with you.

1 Thessalonians 5:28

Recognising grace gets difficult when suffering puts its goggles on us. God does not change, no matter what we are going through. It's a lesson I've learned, am still learning, and may never fully learn in this lifetime. God may not always change my circumstances, but even within that acknowledgement, my circumstances *cannot* change God. Grace still abounds. Grace still cries out from the cross and laughs from the empty tomb. I pray only that I would be given the eyes to see it when all else seems dark.

Grace is not just something we are to receive, but that we are to display – reflectors, bearers of grace. Again, even in painful, difficult or just plain irritating circumstances. The challenge is to be gracious even then; because that's the whole point of grace. It's not reliant on deservedness. Grace is a beautiful reaction to unbeautiful things. It's not a particularly appropriate response in the eyes of the world. But we are called by our God of grace to be gracious. To forgive as he forgave us. To love each other as he has loved us. Are our lives marked with grace? Do we act graciously even when all those around us are being ungracious? How can we bear witness to the grace we have received? For in spite of all our forgetfulness and faithlessness, God remembers us and is always faithful.

> *Increase my awareness of you, Holy Spirit.*
> *Open up my heart;*
> *blow away the dust.*
> *Shatter my chains and unclip my wings.*
> *Remind me of what has gone before*
> *and show me what I have not yet seen.*
> *De-cloud my eyes.*
> *Come, Holy Spirit,*
> *and fill me to the brim,*
> *so that I may embody*
> *the grace of God.*

FOR REFLECTION

- Make an effort to notice what's going on around you, to feel and experience the moment. Take it further and consider where God, through the Spirit, may be showing you something, or simply allow yourself to dwell on thoughts of God – being mindful of God. You may want to write in a journal or share regularly with friends, in order to help you remember these moments.
- Look at the definition of grace you wrote for chapter 11. What might you want to add, or amend?

I remember the days of old,
I think about all your deeds,
I meditate on the works of your hands.
I stretch out my hands to you;
my soul thirsts for you like a parched land.
Psalm 143:5–6

Chapter 21
Choosing to Remember

Remember Jesus Christ, raised from the dead...
2 Timothy 2:8a

If the Spirit of him who raised Jesus from the dead dwells in you, he who raised Christ from the dead will give life to your mortal bodies also through his Spirit that dwells in you.

Romans 8:11

Looking Back

As we've journeyed through this book, we've considered what it means to forget God in our lives, and how we are called to remember God. We've looked at the things that pull our attention from him and prevent us from being mindful of his presence. Some of us will relate to one distracting or disturbing element more than others, and we will all have different ways of dealing with things.

We've seen how this God-forgetting is not just an issue for us in today's world. Forgetfulness occurs across generations and throughout our lives. It takes on cultural forms and is influenced by current realities. But underlying it all is a tendency to forget God, to attempt to replace him with gods we make for ourselves, to walk in the wrong direction. The people of God – past and present – often get caught in the web of forgetfulness.

Forgetfulness sometimes changes its clothes, but the heart of the matter remains the same. We get distracted from the one we claim to serve, worship and follow, and our memories get diluted. We risk missing the signs of his presence, because we spend so little time seeking it. We risk half-hearted toddling behind instead of running to follow the one who calls us. We let other memory makers overpower us and become the scriptwriters of our daily lives. We forget how much God loves us, as we engage in our constant inner dialogues – whether these puff us up or tear us down. Neither is reflective of our calling. Our minds are so busy with other things that we never take the time to rehearse what we've learned about our God and Saviour.

We've also considered how our forgetfulness affects others, and that our call to remember God is not merely about fact retention or lip service but is all bundled up in how we live and reflect God's character to the world. If we close our eyes to injustice or act unfairly or cruelly towards others, we are not God-remembering, we are God-forgetting.

We've also looked at some possible 'helps' – things that might aid us in remembering better – how we can get deeper into our faith, harness the power of association and attention, how we can identify and choose whether the things that go on around us act as distractions or as opportunities to live as God wants us to, in ever increasing spheres of life.

Looking Forward

'The thief comes only to steal and kill and destroy. I came that they [my sheep] may have life, and have it abundantly.'

John 10:10

Remembering is a choice we can make every day. It's easy to forget, then berate ourselves for our forgetfulness, but still keep on forgetting. Nurturing a remembering heart in the face of this chronic, wearying forgetfulness can be a challenge, but it is a necessary one if we are to inhabit the abundant life we have been so graciously given.

This abundant living isn't only for some distant future, but often we approach each day as if it were. Just as we wait to wear a beautiful item of clothing until a special occasion arrives, we can get stuck in the moment of the not-yet-here in our Christian lives. We neglect to act lovingly, to follow wholeheartedly, to celebrate the life God has offered us. We often think of faith and hope as abstract concepts, rather than being elements of something solid and achingly real.

We don't wear our best 'clothes'; we carry on using our old wardrobes, wearing the same old habits, attitudes and false beliefs we've always carried. We forget all those beautiful new clothes we were given when we were 'clothed with Christ' (Galatians 3:27). It's interesting that in John 17, when Jesus prayers to his Father, he offers a definition of eternal life:

> *...this is eternal life, that they may know you, the only true God, and Jesus Christ whom you have sent.*
>
> John 17:3

This description of the nature of eternal life is all about knowing God. The essence of it is not a ticket to a future reality, or a promise of present prosperity or worldly happiness, but an invitation to get to know our Maker in a profound way. A way only made possible by the actions of Jesus and the presence of the Holy Spirit. This knowing may not yet be full-blown, face-to-face knowledge, for we currently only know in part.[46] But this partial knowledge is part of a getting-to-know journey, journeying into a new kind of knowledge which is so much deeper than the dictionary definition of the word.

By remembering previous points along the journey, and by building on them, we are offered something extraordinary. Yet so often we don't bother to take hold of it, chase after it, stick with it. Like some of Jesus' listeners, we turn away because it feels too hard. We go back to our old wardrobe and pull out our old clothes.

We don't always realise we're doing this, and once again memory is a key to helping us. We need reminding of who we are and who we're called to be; we need reminding of the vastness of God's love and grace; we need reminding that Kingdom-living is supposed to start now. When the words have become over-familiar and over-used, perhaps even feeling clichéd, we need reminding that the reality behind them is as fresh and vibrant as it has ever been.

In our new wardrobe we find love, forgiveness, kindness. We find oodles and oodles of grace. To mix the analogies, we find the fruit of the Spirit waiting to be worn and nurtured in our lives. It's all in there, and it's not in separate boxes. It's all part of our many-stranded lives.

Strands of Memory

The process of memory, as we recall events, is constantly adapting and re-adapting, applying and reapplying. It is not a static thing but a dynamic, evolving element in our lives. We need to be aware of both its strength and its weaknesses, allowing ourselves to enjoy remembering without letting memories rule our lives and those of others. Memory, for all its potency, is not God.

[46] See 1 Corinthians 13:12.

Remembering in Scripture is always directed towards God. It's not merely a past event but a present reality, being mindful of God at work in every part of our lives, using memory to chasten us, inspire us and to celebrate where we are now – today.

Remembering is a choice, bundled up with thankfulness and faithfulness and love. We can't box them all up separately. They overlap, one fuelling another, generating a response within us. Remembering is just one facet of our faith, and yet it permeates it. Perhaps a better analogy is that of a strand – one strand interwoven with all the other aspects of our faith identity, but a strand that helps to keep them together, that helps prevent fraying and unravelling. We want to find ways of keeping this strand from breaking, ways of strengthening it and noticing its impact on our lives. Nonetheless, in the end, with all the possible techniques and reminders, I am left with the most important thing. I go to the Master of Remembering – how vast is the sum of his thoughts![47] I say: *Help*. I forget. I forget all the time. Help me to remember.

The Memory Giver
... the Spirit searches everything, even the depths of God.
1 Corinthians 2:10b

Those who counsel or guide us will both show us new things and remind us of what we already know. They will point back to moments of revelation and understanding, make references to words we have already heard and to experiences we have already had. They will point out things we've never noticed before.

The Holy Spirit is our counsellor and our guide, coming alongside us, expressing what we cannot, and reminding us of what we have learned – particularly the teaching and the actions of Jesus, God with us. The Spirit nudges our memories so that the old becomes new again as we turn it over in our minds, retell our stories and apply them in different ways.

The living Spirit of God is no mere memento or souvenir but is an animate, speaking, loving and grieving presence bringing us into the deeper realities of what God has in store for us. The Spirit is not a mechanism but an agent, urging us to go deeper, to keep on remembering and to live our lives fuelled by a constant calling-to-mind of all that God is, all that God has done for us and all God

47 Psalm 139:17.

has made us to be. The Spirit is the Divine Revealer, whispering God into our lives. It is the Spirit on whom we depend when our mental faculties deteriorate or our memories fail us – we have someone who will continue to whisper to us and intercede for us, expressing our wordlessness, helping us in our weakness – including the weakness of failing memories.

It is the Spirit who aids our remembering of God and God-things, crying against the mediocrity of our forgetfulness, drawing us towards our fierce and tender Saviour. The Spirit is the one who gives us a sense of true identity when the world clamours to shrink us to fit an uninspiring, imprisoning mould. The Spirit is the one who frees us from the slavery to fear, and helps us remember who we are.

Not only this, but by encounter and experience of the Spirit, God can create new memories in us – stretching our imaginations and challenging the worldviews, traditions and definitions of faith that we carry with us. The Spirit is the one who transforms and reshapes us, illuminating the false memories we accumulate in this broken world, and breathing in the new, true memory of a God who loves us and values us, who redeems us and brings us out of darkness.

The Spirit is the one who brings healing to the murky places in our hearts, transforming the aching, the weary, the bleeding. The Spirit attunes us to Christ, enabling us to grow into his likeness. The Spirit always remembers.

I ask for the memory giver to soften my heart, to unstop my ears, to tell me the things I used to know, or have only ever known in part. Being in tune with the Spirit of Christ will help me to remember. When my mind is fractured by memory loss, and my heart a mass of faulty remembering, I trust and pray that the memory giver will still whisper, drawing me closer to the heart of God. I pray that however muddled I become, I will still reach for God as my one, my only redeemer.

Open my heart to you, O God;
transform my mind.
Give me the strength and grace I need
to remember you.
May I remember you
in thought and in action.
May I remember you

when I'm by myself
and when I'm with others.
May I remember you
in my attitudes and inclinations.
May I remember you
always.

FOR REFLECTION

- If this book has inspired you, note down some of your impressions. What, in particular, would you like to remember/ actively recall?
- We've been reflecting on the need to remember God in a distracted world. Can you think of some points of action arising from these reflections?

FORGETTING THE FORMER THINGS

On that day,
when remembering is no longer necessary,
I will see you face to face –
such astonishing radiance,
burning away all previous scars and sadness.

On that day,
I will forget the former things
in the face of such incredible newness
all things remade, restored, regained…

On that day,
I will understand what salvation really is
that it's not about running away, but running to the one
who reaches out to me, recreates me, reclaims me.

On that day,
when I am utterly, utterly yours
there will be no need to try and remember.
I will know you, live and breathe your presence…

On that day,
memory will morph into something more wonderful still
as past, present and future collide
the whole story blazing in such vivid relevance
and yet,
barely begun.